The Element Way: Serving, Leading, and Building Teams

A Guide for Team Element at Element Church

By Pastor Erik Lawson

Copyright @ 2025, Erik Lawson

All rights reserved. No part of this book may be reproduced, stored, or transmitted by any means—whether auditory, graphic, mechanical, or electronic—without written permission of both publisher and author, except in the case of brief excerpts used in critical articles and reviews. Unauthorized reproduction of any part of this work is illegal and punishable by law.

Because of the dynamic nature of the Internet, any web addresses or links contained in this book may have changed since publication and may no longer be valid.

Paperback ISBN-13: 979-8-9868682-5-7

First edition published in 2025.
Published in the United States.

Visit the author's website at:
http://www.eriklawson.com/

Published by 415 Leadership Inc.
100 Mall Parkway, Suite 500
Wentzville, Missouri 63385

Table of Contents

Foreword v
Chapter 1: Called to Carry the Mission...........1
Chapter 2: The Heart of "Everyone Matters" .15
Chapter 3: Laugh — Leading with Joy 23
Chapter 4: Excellence That Reflects Jesus 27
Chapter 5: Membership — Connection, Commitment, and Contribution 45
Chapter 6: Equipping the Saints..................63
Chapter 7: Next — What Is Next 83
Chapter 8: Speaking Truth with Grace 105
Chapter 9: Stewardship — Faithfully Managing Time, Talent, and Treasure......................131
About the Author 221

Foreword

When I founded Element Church and launched it in January 2006 with a group of just 30 people, we carried a simple yet powerful vision: ***"Everyone, Everywhere."***

Since then, God has done more than we could ask or imagine. From that small beginning, we've grown into a church family of over 6,000 people attending multiple locations—each one playing a unique part in what God is building through Element Church. Today, our **MISSION** is as clear as ever:

> **"We create life-changing experiences for everyone, everywhere to know Christ, show Christ, and grow Christ."**

This book was written for you—Team Element—our volunteers, leaders, and staff who make this mission possible every single day. Whether you're serving on the frontlines or behind the scenes, you are part of something bigger than any one of us: a movement of people called by God to serve with love, lead with integrity, and build teams that reflect the heart of Jesus.

At the core of everything we do are our **ELEMENT VALUES**. These values aren't just empty words or motivational slogans we hang on walls—instead they shape our culture, inform our decisions, serve as guard rails, and guide how we treat each other and those we serve. When making decisions these values are our GPS to keep us on course:

- **Everyone** – Everyone matters to God; everyone matters to us.

- **Laugh** – Laughter builds bonds and breaks barriers.

- **Excellence** – Excellence reflects God and reaches people.

- **Membership** – We are created to connect and contribute to a local church.

- **Equip** – We empower people to reach their God-given potential.

- **Next** – We celebrate today while seizing tomorrow.

- **Truth** – We are graciously candid with ourselves and with others.

- **Stewardship** – We honor God when we faithfully treasure people, time, and money.

Each chapter in this guide will walk you through these values—not just what they are, but how we live them out as individuals, as teams, in meetings, creating and executing services, innovating systems, and having difficult conversations. You'll also find practical insight on building healthy teams, leading with clarity, and contributing to the overall strength of Element Church. I believe that as you embody these values you will find your own personal life benefiting as you personally become more like Jesus. These values are His values that He lived while on earth and they continue to be the model of being governed by as King of Kings.

Whether you've just joined Team Element or have been serving for years, we hope *The Element Way* inspires and equips you to continue serving with excellence and joy. We are so thankful for you—for the way you give, love, and lead. You are not just building a church; you are helping to shape eternity.

With heartfelt gratitude,

Erik Lawson
Senior and Founding Pastor, Element Church

Chapter 1: Called to Carry the Mission

Before diving into what we do at Element Church, let's first pause and reflect on why we exist. This is foundational. Everything flows from this truth. At Element Church, we're not just building ministries or programs. We're cultivating a culture—one deeply rooted in the mission of Jesus, propelled by a clear vision, and sustained by values that reflect God's heart. This chapter lays out our Mission, Vision, and Values—not as mere statements to recite, but as truths to live by. These are not just cool motivational slogans you see on office posters like, "Team – together everyone achieves more" or "Goals: Aim low and avoid disappointment." These are the principles that shape how we love, lead, and serve together as the body of Christ. These are the winds in our sails and the North Star by which we stay on course.

Mission – Why we exist
Vision – Where we are going and how we'll get there
Values – What we look like when we get there (our culture)

What Is the Mission of Every Believer?

When Jesus was asked which of the 613 of the Old Testament commandments was the greatest, His response defined the mission for every believer and the local church. Jesus didn't just give a theological answer—He gave a transformational framework for life.

> Jesus said to him, "'You shall love the LORD your God with all your heart, with all your soul, and with all your mind.' This is *the* first and great commandment. And *the* second *is* like it: 'You shall love your neighbor as yourself.' On these two commandments hang all the Law and the Prophets." — *Matthew 22:37-40 (New King James Version NKJV)*

Every believer's mission is to **love God, love people.** That's great — but how do I love God? What does it really mean to love God?

> If someone says, "I love God," and hates his brother, he is a liar; for he who does not love his brother whom he has seen, how can he love God whom he has not seen? — *1 John 4:20 (NKJV)*

Chapter 1: Called to Carry the Mission

Loving God isn't just about our vertical relationship with Him—it's reflected in our horizontal relationship with others. We cannot say we love God and yet neglect or mistreat the people around us. Scripture makes it clear: **we love God by loving others.**

> And the King will answer and say to them, 'Assuredly, I say to you, inasmuch as you did *it* to one of the least of these My brethren, you did *it* to Me.' — *Matthew 25:40 (NKJV)*

Just as a staff member might say, "I love this company," the real test of that love is how they treat the people within the company—its coworkers and its customers. Love for an organization is proven through people, and the same principle applies to our love for God. If we truly love Him, we will love what He loves—and that's people.

When my kids were growing up, I naturally cared about what mattered to them—games, cheerleading, baseball, basketball—you name it. I loved everything they loved with the exception of cats. Why did I care about those things? Because I loved them. In the same way, if we love God, we'll care deeply about what matters to Him—and that means we'll care about people.

And if we love people, we will want them to know the God we love.

> And as He walked by the Sea of Galilee, He saw Simon and Andrew his brother casting a net into the sea; for they were fishermen. Then Jesus said to them, "Follow Me, and I will make you become fishers of men." They immediately left their nets and followed Him.
> — *Mark 1:16-18 (NKJV)*

We might expect Jesus to say, "Follow Me and I'll make you more disciplined, more spiritual, smarter, or more organized." But instead, He says: **"I'll make you become fishers of men."**

Following Jesus means fishing for people.

If I'm not fishing—if I'm not reaching people—then who am I really following?

Element Church Mission

At Element Church, our mission is simple but profound: **"We create life-changing experiences for everyone, everywhere, to know Christ, show Christ, and grow in Christ."** This vision is about people, not programs. Purpose, not just performance.

Chapter 1: Called to Carry the Mission

Creating Life-Changing Experiences

Creativity is not optional—it's part of our spiritual DNA.

> In the beginning God created the heavens and the earth. — *Genesis 1:1 (NKJV)*

We serve a creative God, and as His image-bearers, creativity should be a hallmark of our ministry. Creativity reflects God and reaches people. To fulfill our mission, we must create environments and experiences that engage, inspire, and draw people closer to Jesus. Whether through weekend services, kids' ministry, or youth ministry, these experiences should be imaginative, relevant, and designed to make a lasting impact.

Research shows that without reinforcement, people forget a significant amount of new information quickly: within an hour, 50% is lost; after 24 hours, 70%; and after a week, up to 90%. This means creativity and thoughtful teaching are essential to help people remember and apply what they learn. Jesus modeled this perfectly by using illustrative teaching and meaningful settings.

Jesus Used Illustrative Teaching

> When Jesus came into the region of Caesarea Philippi, He asked His disciples, saying, "Who do men say that I, the Son of Man, am?" So they said, "Some *say* John the Baptist, some Elijah, and others Jeremiah or one of the prophets." — *Matthew 16:13–14 (NKJV)*

What makes this moment powerful is that it took place in Caesarea Philippi—a pagan city filled with idols and known as a spiritual stronghold of darkness. It was considered a gateway to the underworld because of caves and flowing springs believed to lead to the abyss. By choosing this location, Jesus declared that He was the true Son of God, the foundation of His church, and that the forces of darkness would not prevail against it *(Matthew 16:18 NKJV)*. When he said to Peter, "on this rock I will build My Church, and the gates of Hades will not prevail against it." He was standing by the cave that was believed to be the entrance to hell. Jesus most likely was pointing to it while He made this statement. This teaches us the importance of context, symbolism, and creativity in making God's truth memorable and impactful.

Chapter 1: Called to Carry the Mission

Life Changing

The heart of the gospel is transformation—Christ came to change us from the inside out. Jesus did not come to just inform your life but to transform it! Every experience we create must carry that life-changing power. As Jesus declared in Luke 4:17-20, He read from the book of Isaiah:

> And He was handed the book of the prophet Isaiah. And when He had opened the book, He found the place where it was written: "The Spirit of the Lord *is* upon Me, Because He has anointed Me. To preach the gospel to *the* poor; He has sent Me to heal the brokenhearted, To proclaim liberty to *the* captives And recovery of sight to *the* blind, *To* set at liberty those who are oppressed; To proclaim the acceptable year of the Lord." Then He closed the book… — *Luke 4:17-20 (NKJV)*

This passage reveals the mission of Jesus: to bring healing, freedom, and restoration to all who encounter Him. Our mission as a church is to reflect that same Spirit in every encounter—helping people find hope, healing, and true freedom in Christ. Life change happens when we open hearts to the gospel's power, offering not just words, but tangible experiences of God's grace and love. Every event, every interaction, and every ministry moment should reflect this purpose: to set people free, heal their brokenness, and invite them into the abundant life Jesus came to give.

Everyone, Everywhere — PEOPLE

Our focus is people—not policies, not programs. Jesus consistently confronted the Pharisees because they valued rules more than relationships. Jesus reminded the Pharisees that the rule of the Sabbath was created for man, not man for the rule of the Sabbath (*Mark 2:27 NKJV*).

I remember a man I met at Walmart whom I hadn't seen in a while. He shared about a bad experience he'd had with a church member. Instead of defending, I listened and asked questions. Sometimes, people just need to be heard. While listening I saw that he was hurt by someone who was following rules but not relationship, the law but not love, and put a policy over a person. It was not a Biblical issue that was at the heart of the matter just a church policy. A well-meaning volunteer who didn't step back to see the bigger picture in the handling of this person mis-navigated this conversation and blew this person out of the water. As a result, this person left church (not just our church) but Big "C" church over a volunteer who mismanaged the situation. If you are ever in doubt escalate the situation up for clarity. People first! This volunteer was right in what they said but wrong in what they did. You can be 100% right while being 100% wrong as such was in this case.

Know Christ

Helping people know Christ is an ongoing journey. It's a process that evolves, and our role is to understand it and actively promote it. The question isn't if someone will take the next step—the question is whose role it is to help them find it. The answer is it is your role.

Our mission is to create experiences for life change—where people find their place, fulfill their purpose, and grow in Christ.

Show Christ

> And He Himself gave some *to be* apostles, some prophets, some evangelists, and some pastors and teachers, for the equipping of the saints for the work of ministry, for the edifying of the body of Christ... — *Ephesians 4:11-12 (NKJV)*

Our job is not ministry as much as it is equipping the saints for ministry. Our job isn't just to do ministry ourselves; it's to equip the saints for ministry. Every department may want to hire more staff, but God has given us a better gift—the gift of not enough. Why? Because we don't need more money—we need more saints doing ministry. Developing people takes time and can get messy, but it's worth it. Long-term, raising up leaders strengthens the whole church.

Grow in Christ

There's a difference between growing old and growing up. Growing old happens automatically, but growing up requires intentionality. The pace of the leaders sets the pace for the pack.

Ask yourself: If everyone was like you, what kind of church would we be? Better or worse?

- **Walk** — If everyone read their Bible and prayed like you do, how would that change us?

- **Worship** — As front-row leaders, are we setting the example in service?

- **Generosity** — If everyone tithed like you, would we be stronger?

Chapter 1: Called to Carry the Mission

Our calling is to lead by example—to walk with Christ ourselves so others can follow and grow.

Element Church Values: ELEMENTS

Our values shape the culture we live and lead in. They are more than statements—they're a reflection of who we are becoming as we walk out our mission to love God and love people. These values guide our attitudes, our actions, and our approach to ministry. They define how we serve, lead, and grow together.

Core Value	What It Means	Biblical Foundation
Everyone	Everyone matters to God; everyone matters to us.	And the King will answer and say to them, 'Assuredly, I say to you, inasmuch as you did *it* to one of the least of these My brethren, you did *it* to Me.'" — *Matthew 25:40 (NKJV)*
Laugh	Laughter builds bonds and breaks barriers.	"A merry heart does good, like medicine, But a broken spirit dries the bones." — *Proverbs 17:22 (NKJV)*

Excellence	Excellence reflects God and reaches people.	And whatever you do, do it heartily, as to the Lord and not to men. — *Colossians 3:23 (NKJV)*
Membership	We are created to connect and contribute to a local church.	Now you are the body of Christ, and members individually. — *1 Corinthians 12:27 (NKJV)*
Equip	We empower people to reach their God-given potential.	And He Himself gave some *to be* apostles, some prophets, some evangelists, and some pastors and teachers, for the equipping of the saints for the work of ministry… — *Ephesians 4:11–12 (NKJV)*

Chapter 1: Called to Carry the Mission

Next	We celebrate today while seizing tomorrow.	Brethren, I do not count myself to have apprehended; but one thing *I do*, forgetting those things which are behind and reaching forward to those things which are ahead… — *Philippians 3:13 (NKJV)*
Truth	We are graciously candid with ourselves and others.	…but, speaking the truth in love, may grow up in all things into Him who is the head— Christ— — *Ephesian 4:15 (NKJV)*
Stewardship	We honor God when we faithfully treasure people, time, and money.	Do not lay up for yourselves treasures on earth, where moth and rust destroy and where thieves break in and steal; but lay up for yourselves treasures in heaven… — *Matthew 6:19–21 (NKJV)*

Our values are the culture we carry—what we look like when we get there. This chapter isn't the finish line—it's the starting point. It's not just about what Element Church believes; it's about who *you* are becoming as a follower of Jesus and a builder in His Church.

So lean in. This is your moment. Carry the mission—because lives are on the other side of your "yes." You're not here by accident. Just as Esther, "You are here for *such* a time as this." *(Esther 4:14 NKJV)* God placed you in this church, on this team, in this season, to be a part of His mission—to fish for people, to create environments for life change, and to build a culture where people are equipped, empowered, and released into purpose.

Chapter 2: The Heart of "Everyone Matters"

Everyone - *Everyone matters to God; everyone matters to us.*

Team, this value—*Everyone Matters*—is not just a statement or a slogan. It's the very heartbeat of who we are at Element Church. Every single person who walks through our doors matters deeply to God, and therefore, they matter deeply to us. I want us to never forget this truth: every individual carries immense worth and dignity. As leaders and ministers, it's our responsibility to honor that truth in every interaction—whether with first-time guests or lifelong members. Our unity as a church family depends on our commitment to this.

Jesus set the example for us. He didn't just notice people; He valued them. He saw the marginalized, the broken, the overlooked—and He made them a priority. We are called to do the same. Every greeting you give, every conversation you lead, every moment you steward is an opportunity to reflect God's love by affirming the sacred worth of the people we serve. There are NO nobodies in this church. Just as every unseen organ in the body is vital, every person here is essential. The ones that are sick are the ones that are often most vital. None of us are insignificant. This truth challenges us to dismantle any biases and to build genuine bridges, so everyone feels truly seen and welcomed.

Making Every Person Somebody

Everyone matters—often, the most important roles are the ones unseen. Think of the liver or kidneys: essential, though invisible. That's how we see people—indispensable, whether visible or not. There are NO nobodies—everyone is a somebody. Think about the human body. The liver, the kidneys—these vital organs work quietly, often unnoticed. But they're indispensable. That's how we view every person here—*no nobodies, only somebodies*. Yet, it's impossible to make someone feel like a somebody if deep down, we think of them as a nobody. How we treat guests is critical—it shapes their entire impression of Element Church.

Every smile you share, every handshake, every kind word says, *you belong here.* Whether it's someone visiting for the first time or someone who's been part of this family for years, their presence is a gift. And they have a place here.

Proverbs remind us of a harsh reality we must resist:

Chapter 2: The Heart of "Everyone Matters"

> Many entreat the favor of the nobility, and every man *is* a friend to one who gives gifts. All the brothers of the poor hate him; How much more do his friends go far from him! He may pursue *them* with words, *yet* they abandon *him*. — *Proverbs 19:6-7 (NKJV)*

We must rise above this kind of rejection in our church. No one should ever feel left behind or forgotten here.

Following Jesus' Example

Sometimes, we may be tempted to prioritize people who can "do something" for the ministry—those who are rich, famous, or powerful. But Jesus shows us a different way.

Consider this man from Mark 5:

> Then they came to the other side of the sea, to the country of the Gadarenes. And when He had come out of the boat, immediately there met Him out of the tombs a man with an unclean spirit, who had *his* dwelling among the tombs; and no one could bind him, not even with chains, because he had often been bound with shackles and chains. And the chains had been pulled apart by him, and the shackles broken in pieces;

> neither could anyone tame him. And always, night and day, he was in the mountains and in the tombs, crying out and cutting himself with stones. — Mark 5:1-5 (NKJV)
>
> Now when Jesus had crossed over again by boat to the other side, a great multitude gathered to Him... — Mark 5:21 (NKJV)

Jesus traveled all night by boat to reach this one man in need. Jesus uses things and loves people. We tend to love things and use people. Jesus reached out first to the hurting, the outcast, and the broken. This is our model.

> On the same day, when evening had come, He said to them, "Let us cross over to the other side." — Mark 4:35 (NKJV)

Jesus had a clear mission: people. He used a boat to reach them, a meal to teach them, time to be with them—but He never confused the value of things with the value of people. Jesus uses things to accomplish kingdom purposes, but He loves people. That's the heart of His ministry. That should be the heart of ours.

We Tend to Get It Backwards. The truth is, we often flip this. We love things—comfort, image, control—

Chapter 2: The Heart of "Everyone Matters"

and unintentionally use people to maintain them. Our culture rewards what we call **B.I.A.S.**—

- **B**eautiful
- **I**nfluential
- **A**ffluent
- **S**uccessful

But Jesus never led with those values. He crossed the sea not to impress, but to impact. Not to gain influence, but to give it away. The disciples thought they were just going to the other side. Jesus knew they were stepping into purpose.

As leaders, we're called to do the same. We go where Jesus leads, even if it's inconvenient, stormy, or uncertain. We measure our leadership not by what we build, but by how well we love. Let's use resources, systems, and strategies—but never at the expense of people. Let's love deeply, lead humbly, and cross over to the other side—because people are waiting there, and Jesus is already in the boat.

Every Interaction Counts

As leaders, we must commit to valuing every moment:

- Every phone call is an opportunity to show care.
- Every email deserves thoughtful attention.
- Every question is a chance to listen and learn.
- Every piece of feedback is a gift for growth.
- Every visitor deserves a warm welcome.
- Every person who is absent is truly missed.
- Every person who has left deserves understanding and grace.

This is how we reflect God's love—and how we build a church family where all truly belong.

Answering the Deepest Question: Do I Matter?

Jesus made this clear when a leper came to Him, kneeling:

> "If You are willing, You can make me clean." Then Jesus, moved with compassion, stretched out *His* hand and touched him, and said to him, "I am willing; be cleansed." — Mark 1:40-41 (NKJV)

Three key takeaways: Jesus answers the deepest question we all ask: *Am I valuable?*

Chapter 2: The Heart of "Everyone Matters"

He breaks societal barriers by touching the unclean calling us to love without partiality. *(James 2:1–4 NKJV).*

He shows us that presence and compassion matter more than words alone. Though Jesus told the healed leper to keep quiet, the man couldn't keep silent—and crowds came running. *(Mark 1:43-45 NKJV)* Word of mouth is powerful. Ninety percent of people trust recommendations from those they know. When we genuinely touch lives, those touched become ambassadors for our church.

As Bill Gates says: "Unhappy customers are your greatest opportunity." Let's listen carefully and respond with grace. This is how we grow in excellence and faithfulness.

Simple, Practical Ways to Live This Out

- Greet everyone with a sincere, warm "Hello."

- Smile genuinely.

- Remember and use people's names—they're powerful.

- Ask thoughtful questions to show you care.

- Listen attentively and engage fully.

These small actions send a huge message: *You belong here.*

Serving with Honor

Remember, guests are why we're here. One bad experience can turn someone away. But our attitude, our enthusiasm, can draw them in.

- Step forward eagerly. Walk with guests, don't just point the way.
- Be honest. If you don't know something, admit it—and find the answer.
- Always speak respectfully about others, especially in their presence.

Serving with excitement, integrity, and honor creates a welcoming atmosphere where everyone feels valued.

Everyone Matters isn't just a phrase—it's a calling God has placed on us. Every person who enters our doors carries immense worth because God loves them deeply. As leaders, we are entrusted to reflect that love through genuine care, warm welcome, and meaningful connection. Let's live this truth every day—not only through big gestures but through countless small, intentional acts of kindness.

Chapter 3: Laugh — Leading with Joy

Laugh – *Laughter builds bonds and breaks barriers.*

Laughter isn't a distraction from leadership—it's a vital part of it. In ministry, where burdens can be heavy and days long, joy is more than a nice-to-have—it's a spiritual strength. This chapter explores how laughter reflects the heart of Jesus, builds healthy teams, and sustains us in the work we're called to. Let's rediscover the power of joy in leadership.

The Healing Power of Laughter

Laughter is more than just fun—it's life-giving and healing. As *Proverbs 17:22 (NKJV)* says,

> **A merry heart does good, *like* medicine,**
> **But a broken spirit dries the bones.**

I once read about a man diagnosed with a terminal illness who decided, "If I'm going to die, I might as well die laughing." So, he watched comedies like *The Three Stooges* daily. When he returned to his doctor, his illness was reportedly gone. Laughter had become a part of his healing journey.

> The thief does not come except to steal, and to kill, and to destroy. I have come that they may have life, and that they may have *it* more abundantly.— *John 10:10 (NKJV)*

Jesus Was Joyful

Jesus came to give us life. He was accused of being the life of the party. Sinners loved being around Jesus. Now He never sinned or compromised but I believe he was full of joy and wasn't uptight all the time. Pharisees were uptight, "Jesus said you strain gnats and swallow camels."

> Then little children were brought to Him that He might put *His* hands on them and pray, but the disciples rebuked them. But Jesus said, "Let the little children come to Me, and do not forbid them; for of such is the kingdom of heaven." And He laid *His* hands on them and departed from there. — *Matthew 19:13-15 (NKJV)*

Most people aren't rejecting Jesus but are turned off by Christians' poor representation of Him. Kids loved Jesus. If Jesus had been scary, crusty, and uptight, they would have backed away. You've seen kids scream when they're placed on Santa's lap for a photo—now imagine the opposite with Jesus. Children were drawn to Him.

Practicing Joy and Laughter Together

In my Executive Team meetings, we intentionally build in 10 minutes at the start for personal time. Usually, we tell jokes, share stories, or watch funny videos together. It's a chance to laugh and connect before tackling serious matters.

We also prioritize fun days for staff. These help us build stronger bonds beyond the work environment. Sometimes we play games, have outings, or do team-building activities that bring joy and laughter.

Laugh at Yourself

One of the best pieces of advice I've learned is: laugh at yourself. Others already are, so why not join them? It helps you not to take yourself too seriously.

Joy Needs Rest

Don't forget to take breaks. Go for a walk, watch a good movie, play a game, or read a relaxing book. Sabbath rest is God's design for us, not a legalistic rule. It refreshes and renews us to lead well.

Leading with Joy Is Ministry

Laughter and joy are ministries in themselves. They break down barriers, build authentic relationships, and reflect the vibrant life of Christ. Serving with joy—even in hard times—demonstrates the hope and love Jesus offers. This joy invites people into an environment where they feel safe, welcomed, and deeply valued. May laughter fill your home, your team meetings, and your ministry spaces. Let joy be your strength as you lead others into the abundant life Christ offers.

Laughter isn't the opposite of seriousness—it's the overflow of grace, connection, and trust. When we lead with joy, we reflect the heart of Jesus and create environments where people feel safe, seen, and refreshed. Don't underestimate the ministry of a smile, a shared joke, or a light-hearted moment in the middle of a busy day. Joy is contagious. Let it start with you.

The book of Jude written by the half-brother of Jesus is 1 chapter *(Matt. 13:55 and Gal. 1:19)*, and it is power packed with truth. **The strength of a chapter is not reflected by the length of it.** Although this is a short chapter, I believe it's a power pacted one and vital for our culture.

Chapter 4: Excellence That Reflects Jesus

Excellence – *Excellence reflects God and reaches people.*

Have you ever walked into a place and immediately felt, "They really care here"? I am sure you have had the opposite experience more often, and that is to walk into a place, and you can tell, "They really don't care." Excellence communicates value without a word. A lack of excellence without a word spoken communicates "You don't matter, and we don't care." In this chapter, we'll discover how excellence isn't just about performance, but about reflecting the nature of Jesus and helping people feel seen and honored.

Excellence is not about perfection—it's about devotion. It's not performance—it's worship. At Element Church, excellence is more than a core value. It's how we show the world what God is like. Every time you volunteer—whether on stage, behind the scenes, or in a quiet moment of service—you are making a bold declaration: **our God is worthy of our very best.** This chapter unpacks why excellence matters in everything we do. From biblical examples like Daniel, Joseph, and

Solomon, to daily tasks in our church family, we'll see how excellence reflects God's nature and helps us reach people with His love.

Excellence Is Our Calling

We serve a God of excellence. Creation didn't happen halfway. Salvation didn't stop short. The cross wasn't partial—it was complete.

> Then this Daniel distinguished himself above the governors and satraps, because an excellent spirit *was* in him; and the king gave thought to setting him over the whole realm. — *Daniel 6:3 (NKJV)*

> And his master saw that the Lord *was* with him and that the Lord made all he did to prosper in his hand. So Joseph found favor in his sight, and served him. Then he made him overseer of his house… — *Genesis 39:3-4 (NKJV)*

From the Old Testament to today, God honors those who lead and serve with excellence. I believe we're not just building a great church—we're showing the world the greatness of our God. That means we don't cut corners. We don't settle. And we don't stop halfway.

Excellence Reflects God

The opposite of excellence would be mediocre which means half-way up the stoney mountain. God didn't meet with Moses halfway up the mountain but on top.

- God didn't meet Moses halfway—He called him to the top.

- Jesus didn't go halfway to the cross—He went all the way.

We don't serve a halfway God. So, we won't be a halfway church. If "99.9% were good enough" here would be the disastrous results:

- 2,000,000 IRS documents lost each year

- 22,000 wrong bank withdrawals every 60 minutes

- 12 babies given to the wrong parents daily

- 20,000 incorrect drug prescriptions in one year

If that's unacceptable in hospitals and banks, how much more in the church of Jesus? When we lower our standards, it doesn't just reflect on us—it reflects on **Him**.

The Cost of Mediocrity

In business, mediocrity costs profit. In the church, **mediocrity costs people**. I've met people who left church because they emailed, and no one responded. Or they called with a need and were ignored. That breaks my heart—and yes, it makes my blood boil. Why? Because Jesus leaves the 99 to go after the one. And we never want to be the kind of church that lets "the one" fall through the cracks.

Small lapses can have negative eternal consequences:

- A missed call

- An unanswered email

- A poor guest experiences

- A detail forgotten or overlooked

People don't just leave churches because of theology—they leave because they feel unseen, unheard, or unimportant. Let's be clear: Excellence is compassion in action. When we follow up, follow through, and follow Christ's example, we're telling people they matter.

We Represent Jesus

Let me ask you this: What does it say to an unchurched person if businesses operate with more excellence to make sales than we do to reach souls? We are carriers of Christ. His ambassadors. For some, we are the only version of Jesus they will ever see. So, what do they see in us? A God who is sloppy? Distracted? Unprepared? Or a God who is worthy of their trust, attention, and devotion?

Jesus didn't go halfway to the cross. Therefore, we as believers and as a church will not go halfway in taking the message of the cross to the world.

What Is Excellence?

So…what *is* excellence? First, let's start by answering the question of what excellence is not. It is not perfection because that is only attainable by God. The pursuit of perfection is the enemy of progress. The best definition of excellence I know is "doing the best you can with where you are and what you have."

It can be hard to define in detail, but you *know* what it is when you see it—and you definitely know when you don't. Take the Belgian army officer entrance exam. There are 85 questions... and you only need to get 20 right to pass. Nobody's too worried about an invasion from Belgium anytime soon. But if they do attack, I'd stock up on syrup. They might catapult us with waffles or something.

Booker T. Washington said, "Excellence is to do a common thing in an uncommon way."

Excellence isn't an unlimited supply of money to do big things. It is simply doing the little things with that little extra that sets it apart from ordinary. That little extra makes a big difference. Excellence isn't about being perfect—because perfect isn't attainable. It's a little more!

That "little extra" makes a big difference. It's not about being perfect—because perfect isn't attainable. Excellence is about doing just a little *more* than expected. At 211 degrees, water is hot. At 212 degrees, it turns into steam—powerful enough to drive a locomotive or move a steamship across the ocean. That's the difference of *one degree*. And that's what excellence looks like: small shifts with big impact.

Chapter 4: Excellence That Reflects Jesus

Excellence in Action: Four Traits

#1 Do the Little Things Just a Little Better

Here's where excellence starts—small things, done just a bit better:

- Showing up on time

- Starting the meeting on time

- Being prepared for the meeting

- Correct spelling in publications

(I can relate to what President Andrew Jackson said: "It's a poor mind indeed that can't think of at least two ways of spelling a word." I can usually think of three.)

- Returning phone calls promptly

- Smiling while you talk to others

- Greeting guests with warmth—as they walk in, not just when they reach you

- Not just pointing someone to an aisle—walk them there

- Following through on what you say

None of this is glamorous. But this is what builds trust, hospitality, and consistency—and helps people experience Christ in the details.

#2 Pay Attention to Detail

A young businesswoman was opening a new store. A friend sent a floral arrangement to celebrate the grand opening. But when he arrived, he was horrified to see the ribbon read: "Rest in peace." He immediately called the florist. After apologizing, the florist said: "Well, look at it this way—somewhere today a man was buried under a wreath that said, 'Good luck in your new location.'"

Details matter.

When I think of details I think of Disney. The inspiration to build Disney theme parks came when Walt took his little girls to an amusement park. From a distance the carousal looked beautiful as it spun around in circles. However, when he got up close and the carousal stopped spinning, he saw that all the paint was chipped, and the horses didn't move up and down. He thought to himself, "One day I will create a place where the paint never chips, and all the horses jump." And today we enjoy Disney World from Florida, to California, and Shanghai and Tokyo, Japan and more. Thank you, Mr. Disney, for not settling for mediocrity.

#3 Put Your Heart Into It

Studies say:

- 85% of U.S. workers believe they could work harder if they wanted to

- Over 50% say they could double their effectiveness

That's not a skill issue—it's a heart issue. In the church, heart matters. We don't serve to impress people—we serve because we're serving Jesus.

> And whatever you do, do it heartily, as to the Lord and not to men, knowing that from the Lord you will receive the reward of the inheritance; for you serve the Lord Christ. *Colossians — 3:23–24 (NKJV).*

Serving with excellence starts with a heart posture of worship and purpose.

#4 Keep Working On It

One of the most winning NBA coaches was Pat Riley. He once said: "Excellence is the gradual result of always striving to do better." Excellence is a moving target. What is excellent for us today will not be excellence for us next month. Today's excellence will be tomorrow's mediocre. That's why we don't settle. Architect Frank Lloyd Wright, at age 83, was asked what he considered to be his greatest masterpiece. He replied: "My next one." That's the attitude we want in ministry—humble, hungry, always improving.

Excellence That Attracts, Tests, and Answers

When people walk through the doors of your church, your team, your ministry—what do they see? What do they experience? What do they remember? Excellence matters. Because excellence doesn't just impress—it reveals the wisdom and glory of God. In 1 Kings 10, the Queen of Sheba traveled more than 1,500 miles—possibly from Yemen or Ethiopia—to see Solomon. But it wasn't just Solomon's wisdom that drew her in—it was his excellence, and even more, it was his God.

Chapter 4: Excellence That Reflects Jesus

> Now when the queen of Sheba heard of the fame of Solomon concerning the name of the Lord, she came to test him with hard questions. — *1 Kings 10:1 (NKJV)*

Let's look at three things excellence does: It attracts, it tests, and it answers.

#1 Excellence Attracts

Sheba didn't come because of Instagram reels or clever ads—she heard a report. And not just about Solomon—but about his fame connected to the name of the Lord. People will come when they hear the fame of Jesus. The greatest advertisement is word of mouth.

- The best church growth strategy isn't marketing—it's making Jesus famous.

- Word of mouth is powerful—if someone is talking about your ministry, what are they saying? And trust me when I say that 35 years of ministry has taught me people are talking whether you like it or not. What matters is what they are saying! Fortunately, excellence can help influence what they say.

- When excellence reflects God's glory, people will come from far away.

She made a 1,500-mile journey based on what she'd heard. What are people hearing about our house?

#2 Excellence Will Be Tested

She didn't come to be entertained—she came to test. Every visitor, every newcomer, every returning guest is testing us. Like a test drive, they're asking:

- Is this place real?

- Do they really care?

- Are they organized?

- Are they joyful?

- Does the presence of God really live here?

She came to Jerusalem with a very great retinue, with camels that bore spices, very much gold, and precious stones; and when she came to Solomon, she spoke with him

> about all that was in her heart. — *1 Kings 10:2 (NKJV)*

Resources and relationships for ministry are with the people coming in our front door. Jesus paid temple tax. He told Peter to go fish, and a coin was in the fish's mouth. Do you need more money for ministry *(Matt. 17:27 NKJV)*? It's in the fish we are catching.

Let's not be a catch and release church!

> So Solomon answered all her questions; there was nothing so difficult for the king that he could not explain *it* to her. — *1 Kings 10:3 (NKJV)*

We don't pass the test with production—we pass it with presence. People don't expect perfection—but they do expect authenticity, warmth, humility, and help.

The people God is sending through your front door carry what you need for ministry—relationships, resources, wisdom, capacity. Just like in *Matthew 17:27*, when Jesus told Peter to go fish and find a coin in its mouth to pay the temple tax, the provision was in the catch.

#3 Excellence Answers

> So Solomon answered all her questions; there was nothing so difficult for the king that he could not explain *it* to her." — *1 Kings 10:3 (NKJV)*

We must be a church that answers the questions people are actually asking.

- Are they leaving with hope?

- Are they leaving with clarity?

- Or are they leaving more confused than they came?

People don't just need more content. They need truth with grace, wisdom with relevance, and Jesus with skin on. They don't just need information but transformation.

ANSWERS: We are a church that is answering questions people are actually asking.

Do people leave with more questions? Do they leave with questions unanswered?

Chapter 4: Excellence That Reflects Jesus

> And when the queen of Sheba had seen all the wisdom of Solomon, the house that he had built, the food on his table, the seating of his servants, the service of his waiters and their apparel, his cupbearers, and his entryway by which he went up to the house of the Lord, there was no more spirit in her... Happy *are* your men and happy *are* these your servants, who stand continually before you *and* hear your wisdom! — 1 Kings 10:4–5,8 (NKJV)

Wisdom is seen, not just heard. Excellence took her breath away. Excellence removed her excuses, and she was won over to Jehovah. Jesus said, Queen of South will rise up in judgment against this generation. *(Matt. 12:42 NKJV)* An Ethiopian was reading scroll of Isaiah and coming from Jerusalem to worship. *(Acts 8:27 NKJV)* Why? Influence of Sheba was felt hundred's years after her death.

She didn't just hear wisdom—she saw it:

1. **House** – Our facilities reflect our values

2. **Food** – Hospitality matters (does it feel like home?)

3. **Seating of servants** – Organization and intentionality

4. **Service of waiters** – Customer service, volunteer care

5. **Apparel** – Personal appearance and presentation

6. **Cupbearers** – Our leaders

7. **Entryway** – Their walk and their worship

8. **Happy** – Do we love what we do?

She was breathless— "there was no more spirit in her."

Let's commit to excellence—not for our glory, but to make Jesus famous. Let's build with intentionality. Let's answer real questions. Let's treat every guest like royalty. Let's not just catch— we'll disciple, raise up, and release people to their calling. Because excellence doesn't just impress—it impacts.

Excellence is not about impressing people—it's about representing Jesus well. From the parking lot to the platform, every detail speaks. So, let's do the little things a little better. Let's honor people through preparation. Let's never settle for halfway when our Savior went all the way. When we lead

Chapter 4: Excellence That Reflects Jesus

with excellence, we shine the light of Christ—and people will be drawn to Him.

Chapter 5: Membership — Connection, Commitment, and Contribution

Membership – *We are created to connect and contribute to a local church.*

Church membership is more than a card or a weekly attendance number. It's about belonging—being part of a family where connection, commitment, and contribution shape not only our lives but the life of the church.

What Is Biblical Membership?

I've got a lot of memberships—loyalty cards from restaurants, a gym membership, a library card, airport lounges, and a handful of others. Each one gives me access to certain perks, but let's be honest—they don't require much from me. I use them when it's convenient, and if I don't feel like it, I let them sit unused.

Sadly, this is how many people treat church—as if it were just another membership card, like one for the library. Show up when it suits them. Take what they want. Leave quietly. But this is not the biblical model of church membership.

Let's look at what Scripture teaches about what it really means to belong.

> For as we have many members in one body, but all the members do not have the same function, so we, *being* many, are one body in Christ, and individually members of one another. Having then gifts differing according to the grace that is given to us, *let us use them...* — Romans 12:4-6 (NKJV)

The Three Pillars of Membership

Biblical membership is threefold: **Connection, Commitment, and Contribution.**

#1 Connection: Membership means belonging to His body—not just attending as a fan. You were created for deep, life-giving connection to other believers.

#2 Commitment: Membership requires loyalty to one body—not hopping around like a buffet of spiritual preferences. Church is family, where we are rooted, grow, and serve together.

#3 Contribution: Each member has gifts to use. Membership is active, not passive. When everyone contributes, the church thrives.

Why Connection Matters

> So, continuing daily with one accord in the temple, and breaking bread from house to house, they ate their food with gladness and simplicity of heart, praising God and having favor with all the people. And the Lord added to the church daily those who were being saved. — *Acts 2:46–47 (NKJV)*

This joy flows naturally when we move beyond casual attendance into active membership. Gladness and happiness are by-products of commitment, connection, and contribution to the local Church Body. I find it interesting that the very thing that often keeps people from connecting to their local church is that they are out pursuing happiness—only to find it's not out there. I have observed the happiest people I know are not necessarily the richest, world traveling, and successful but those who are simply connected consistently to their local life-giving Church.

God describes us as Sheep. Sheep are a very social animal. In a grazing situation, they need to see other sheep. In fact, ensuring that sheep always have visual contact with other sheep will prevent excess stress when moving or handling them. Animal behaviorists say a group of five sheep is necessary for sheep to display their normal flocking behavior. A sheep becomes highly agitated if it is separated from rest of the flock.

If you only come to church and never connect relationally, you will plateau in happiness. Statistics say 75% of people who attend a church leave after six months if they don't connect with someone relationally. Here is what happens after six months, people leave and then spend 6-12 months looking for another church. Then find one and after 6 months don't connect and leave and repeat the cycle.

At Element, being on staff or serving as a volunteer is more than a job or task. It's not about clocking in or filling a spot. It's about being a team.

- We connect as a team.

- We play as a team.

- We win or lose as a team.

- We grow as a team.

Chapter 5: Membership — Connection, Commitment, and Contribution

There are no lone rangers here. We're not built for that. That means being relationally connected, spiritually committed, and fully engaged in contributing with the gifts God has given you.

Most believe the Christian life is primarily a personal relationship between God and me. We think the most important thing we can do is keep that relationship going strong—by maintaining our quiet times, living holy, and going to church so that we're "fed."

Good. Important. But... not complete.

There's a difference between a <u>personal</u> and <u>private</u> relationship! Christianity was never meant to be lived in isolation.

The First "Not Good"

Do you know the first time in the Bible that God said something was bad? Most people think it was when Adam and Eve sinned, or when they ate from the tree of the knowledge of good and evil. But it was actually much earlier—before sin entered the world.

Go back to the beginning: Adam, the first man, had a perfect personal relationship with God. He spent all his time with the Lord in the Garden of Eden.

There was no sin. His fellowship with God was unbroken. God Himself was "feeding" him. By our definition, this was the ideal relationship.

Yet God says:

> "*It is* not good that man should be alone; I will make him a helper comparable to him."
> — *Genesis 2:18 (NKJV)*

In Hebrew, this phrase "not good" is "lo tob" meaning, "it's bad" for Adam to be alone. The first moment that God says something was not good wasn't when people sinned it was when he saw that Adam was alone. *This teaches us a profound truth:*

God made us with certain needs He chose not to meet.

Designed for One Another

Why did God create Adam with a need for someone else? Because Adam was given a mission:

> "Be fruitful and multiply ($1 \times 0 = 0$); fill the earth and subdue it; have dominion..." — *Genesis 1:28 (NKJV)*

Chapter 5: Membership — Connection, Commitment, and Contribution

You can't do any of this alone! The thing Adam is missing to fulfill this task. A woman. God made us to need others who aren't like us. Our differences are what complete us. We are very different...

That principle continues in the Church today: God made us to need others—especially those who are different than us.

"Pastor, I'm Just Too Busy..."

Here's the reality: The problem is we are busy with things that are of lesser importance. Too often we give *first-class allegiance to second-class causes.* We watch reruns of *Friends* instead of actually making friends. We follow reality shows about other people's families instead of building the reality of our own.

In 2001, a home in Chicago became overgrown and apparently abandoned. When it was auctioned for back taxes, officials entered and discovered the body of Adolph Stick, still sitting in his chair. Next to him, a newspaper dated 1997. He had been dead for four years—and no one noticed. How does someone die—and no one even know?

So, let's ask ourselves: Am I too busy for what Jesus said was most important? Jesus didn't just call us to a private faith. He called us to a shared life, a body, a family. Let's not settle for a personal relationship with Jesus that's disconnected from the people Jesus gave us to walk with.

The Rewards of Team

In the body of Christ, every member matters—and when you find your place on the team, you don't just serve, you thrive. There are powerful rewards to being connected, committed, and united. Let's take a closer look at what happens when we serve together.

Synergy: We Go Further Together

When you find your place on the team you can experience synergy. There is something remarkable that happens when we serve alongside others. It's called *synergy* — *"The interaction or cooperation of two or more organizations, substances, or other agents to produce a combined effect greater than the sum of their separate effects."*

Michael Jordan put it this way: *"Talent wins games, but teamwork wins championships."*

A beautiful example of this is found in nature: geese flying in formation. Researchers discovered that geese flying in the "V" formation can travel 72%

farther than they could alone. The lead goose creates an up current that lifts those behind. When the lead goose gets tired, it rotates to the back, and another takes its place—ensuring the whole team keeps moving forward with less strain.

In the same way, when each of us takes our place in the body, we gain strength from one another—and together, we can go so much farther than we ever could alone.

Safety: We Protect One Another

When you find your place on the team you experience a greater degree of safety. Being part of a team doesn't just help us go further—it also gives us a deeper sense of safety and protection.

The North American Bison provides another powerful image. When wolves attack a weak or sick member of the herd, the strong bison form a circle around the vulnerable one, facing outward. They become a living shield—refusing to let the wounded one be taken.

That's what the church family is meant to do. When our team is hurt, we surround them with love, faith, and prayer. We stick together. When you are hurt or spiritually feeling weak that is when you need the team the most.

Your Unique Contribution Matters

Beyond strength and safety, being on the team gives your life lasting significance. When you find your place on the team, what you do and the position you play, no matter what it is, has eternal impact in the lives of people. So much of what we do in our lives will mean little in eternity let alone five years from now. Why not invest some time into something that will last forever.

When we get to heaven we will see many amazing things, streets of gold, mansions, angels, the tree of life and so on but there is something you will never see again when you get there and that is another non-Christian. Now is the only chance we must tell others about the hope of God's redemptive story that leads to eternal life. When we get to eternity, we will never have another chance to lead someone to Christ.

Sometimes we think our contribution doesn't matter—but history tells us otherwise. Consider this:

- In 1645, **one vote** gave Oliver Cromwell control of England.

- In 1845, **one vote** brought Texas into the Union.

Chapter 5: Membership — Connection, Commitment, and Contribution

- In 1876, **one vote** made Rutherford B. Hayes President of the United States.

Never underestimate the power of one. Your voice. Your service. Your faith. Your presence.

It matters—more than you know.

Commitment: Growth Through the Storm

Membership defined by the Bible is <u>CONNECTION</u>, <u>COMMITMENT</u>, and <u>CONTRIBUTION</u>. We've already explored the value of connection—how being spiritually connected brings health and vitality. Today, let's look deeper into the second pillar of membership: commitment.

If my hand is not connected to my arm, how healthy will it be? If we are members of a body but not connected to a local body, things begin to die in our life. I have never met a Christian who disconnected from a local church body who said, 'It was the best decision I ever made.'

> Those who are planted in the house of the Lord shall flourish in the courts of our God.
> — *Psalms 92:13 (NKJV)*

When you take a plant and keep transplanting it from container to container it might die from shock. The same is true for many believers that keep jumping from church to church or staff to staff.

Years ago, when I was starting out in ministry as an associate youth pastor, it felt like there was *always* a reason to quit. I still remember my first office—it was literally a broom closet. But even then, God was doing something in me. God was more concerned about working on what was inside of me than the room I was inside. God needed to enlarge the inside of my character before enlarging the chair I sat in. I like what Billy Graham often prayed, "Lord never promotes me beyond what my character can handle."

Ministry is not about shiny positions or comfortable surroundings. I've seen people serve for a year or two, then leave as soon as the honeymoon season ends. Rarely have I seen this kind of person go on to flourish somewhere else. Because a change of location doesn't change what's inside of an individual.

Growth doesn't come from comfort—it comes from commitment. When becoming part of a team, there are four stages. Every healthy team goes through four essential stages:

Chapter 5: Membership — Connection, Commitment, and Contribution

- **Forming** – Excitement is high. People are figuring out their roles.

- **Storming** – Conflicts arise. Personalities clash.

- **Norming** – Team chemistry forms. Trust is built.

- **Performing** – The team flows with unity and purpose.

Too often, people leave during the "storming" phase, never making it to the joy of "performing." But storms are part of the journey—they refine us. Jesus talked about two builders: one wise, one foolish. The storm came to *both*. The difference was what they built on. "In times of peace, prepare for war." Crisis doesn't just test your situation—it reveals who you really are:

- **Crisis reveals what you believe** *(your faith)* – just like the disciples panicked in the boat.

- **Crisis reveals who you have become** *(your character)* – it's not just about reacting, but about who you've allowed God to shape you into.

Storms are seasonal—they come, but they also go. Remember Noah? That storm didn't last forever. And after the storm, God began something new through Noah's faithfulness.

Storms Strip Away What Doesn't Matter to Reveal What Does Matter. Storms are a part of life. But they are never without purpose. God uses storms to strip away what doesn't matter and reveal what truly does.

> "Yet once more I shake not only the earth, but also heaven."...that the things which cannot be shaken may remain. Therefore, since we are receiving a kingdom which cannot be shaken, let us have grace, by which we may serve God acceptably with reverence and godly fear." — *Hebrews 12:26b-28 (NKJV)*

In calm seasons, it's easy to focus on the "yards" of our life—the visible things: the car, the lawn décor, the little touches of yard bling that make us feel successful or secure. But when a storm hits, all of that becomes secondary. Suddenly, the only thing that matters is the strength of the house—the structure that protects the people inside. Storms have a way of clarifying our priorities. They remove the distractions so we can rediscover what's eternal.

Chapter 5: Membership — Connection, Commitment, and Contribution

Hunker Down in the Storm.

> "I will say of the Lord, 'He is my refuge and my fortress; My God, in Him I will trust.'"—*Psalm 91:2 (NKJV)*

When the winds rise and the pressure builds, our first instinct might be to run. But the better response is to hunker down—don't run around. Just let it blow over.

Never make a decision to leave while in the storm—likewise, never make major life decisions when in the storm. One of the greatest mistakes we can make is to walk away from where God placed us—just because we're in a storm.

God led you here. Let it be God when it's time to leave—not the storm, not your emotions, not the discomfort.

From Consumer to Contributor

> "For we are His workmanship, created in Christ Jesus for good works, which God prepared beforehand that we should walk in them." — *Ephesians 2:10 (NKJV)*

We live in a culture that often teaches us to ask, *"What can I get out of this?"* But God's design for His Church—and for your life—is not rooted in consumerism. It's grounded in contribution.

You Were Created for More

The Greek word for "created" conveys the idea of ownership by the Maker—like something uniquely designed, copyrighted, and trademarked. You are one of a kind, and there can never be another one made like you. God put a trademark on you.

You are not a copy. You are not a clone. You are an original, handcrafted by the Creator Himself. There will never be another you.

So, the question becomes: Are you living like a consumer or a contributor?

The Dead Sea receives from the Jordan River but has no outlet. It keeps taking in—but never gives out. And because of that, it is lifeless. Many believers fall into the same trap. We attend, we receive, we absorb—but we never pour out. And over time, something in our spirit starts to die.

Three Areas We All Are Called to Contribute

Chapter 5: Membership — Connection, Commitment, and Contribution

If you're wondering where to start, God has already given you the answer. Every one of us can contribute to these three areas:

#1 Time – Your schedule reflects your priorities. We all have the same 24 hours, but how we invest them reveals what we truly value.

#2 Talent – You have gifts, skills, and passions that were given to you for a purpose. Use them. Don't bury them. The Body of Christ needs your part.

#3 Treasure – What you give reveals what you love. You can measure your heart by where your treasure flows.

> "Do not lay up for yourselves treasures on earth, where moth and rust destroy and where thieves break in and steal; but lay up for yourselves treasures in heaven, where neither moth nor rust destroy and where thieves do not break in and steal. For where your treasure is, there your heart will be also." — *Matthew 6:19–21 (NKJV)*

Membership is more than a label—it's a lifestyle. When you connect, commit, and contribute, you become part of something greater than yourself. You help build a church where life is transformed and God's kingdom advances. Let's embrace membership as God designed it and live out our calling together.

Chapter 6: Equipping the Saints

Equip- *We empower people to reach their God-given potential.*

The church grows when every member is empowered to serve. Ministry isn't meant to be done by an elite few, but by many equipped and released. This chapter explores how leaders can move from doing everything themselves to equipping others—fulfilling God's design for a multiplying, thriving church.

From Doing to Equipping

Everyone has a job description (JD) in mind for the pastor and pastoral staff. But most people have the wrong idea of what the pastor's job is. Here's the reality: 80% of churches in the U.S. have fewer than 100 people in attendance—and there's a reason. In many small church mindsets, the pastor is expected to do everything. But is that really what Jesus intended?

Let's look at what the Bible says about the pastor's role.

> And He Himself gave some *to be* apostles, some prophets, some evangelists, and some pastors and teachers, for the equipping of the saints for the work of ministry, for the edifying of the body of Christ, till we all come to the unity of the faith... to a perfect man... may grow up in all things into Him who is the head—Christ—from whom the whole body, joined and knit together by what every joint supplies, according to the effective working by which every part does its share, causes growth of the body for the edifying of itself in love. — *Ephesians 4:11-16 (NKJV)*

This passage makes it clear: the five-fold ministry was given to equip the saints for the work of ministry—not to do all the ministry themselves. If I'm running around trying to do everything myself, I'm missing the purpose God designed for me. Let's see what this looked like in the early church.

Chapter 6: Equipping the Saints

God's Math for Church Growth

#1 Addition

> Then those who gladly received his word were baptized; and that day about three thousand souls were added to *them*. — Acts 2:41 (NKJV)

This moment marked a powerful contrast between the old covenant and the new. Under the law, 3,000 perished because of its demands and inability to grant life, but through the Spirit, that same number were saved. As Paul later wrote, *'The letter kills, but the Spirit gives life.'* This shows the transformative power of the Spirit in bringing true life and growth to the Church.

#2 Subtraction

In Acts 5, Ananias and Sapphira lied to the Holy Spirit about their giving and died before the Lord. God prunes His church. We often talk about "closing the back door" in church growth, but the body has a back door—because not everything that comes in should stay. A body that doesn't pass waste becomes toxic. We are not called to keep everybody.

#3 Church Growth Creates Problems

> Now in those days, when *the number* of the disciples was multiplying, there arose a complaint against the Hebrews by the Hellenists, because their widows were neglected in the daily distribution. — *Acts 6:1 (NKJV)*

As the church multiplied, complaints and divisions began to surface.

#4 Division

Satan has his math plan for the church and that is division: Division always tries to follow growth. But then something shifts.

> Then the word of God spread, and the number of the disciples multiplied greatly in Jerusalem... — *Acts 6:7 (NKJV)*

#5 Multiplication

> Then the twelve summoned the multitude of the disciples and said, "It is not desirable that we should leave the word of God and serve tables. Therefore, brethren, seek out from among you seven men of *good*

> reputation, full of the Holy Spirit and wisdom, whom we may appoint over this business; but we will give ourselves continually to prayer and to the ministry of the word." — *Acts 6:2-4 (NKJV)*

So, what changed? What was the difference maker? They equipped the saints for the work of the ministry. Notice that when the Apostles focused on what they should do and empowered saints to do the work of the ministry the church multiplied.

When leaders equip the people—and stop doing everything themselves—the church grows the way God intended.

Roadblocks To Equipping

> And He Himself gave some *to be* apostles, some prophets, some evangelists, and some pastors and teachers, for the equipping of the saints for the work of ministry, for the edifying of the body of Christ. — *Ephesians 4:11-12 (NKJV)*

If our job is to equip the saints for ministry, then why don't more leaders equip others?

"I Can Do It Better" Attitude

That may be initially true, but if your job is to help others grow and develop their gifts, sometimes settling for less on the front end leads to greater results in the long run.

- **The Mom Example:**
  A mom who never lets her kids clean their own room or do their own laundry will always be tired—and raise kids who don't know how to succeed.

- **The Boss Example**:
  A boss who refuses to delegate because "no one can do it like me" will burn out and push away high-capacity team members. *If you're always overworked, the problem may not be workload—it might be a lack of developing and deploying others.*

- **The Pastor Example**:
  I've developed other pastors on my staff to preach. The #1 complaint I get. "We want *you* to preach more." Truth? I might *do it better (initially)* —but only because I've been doing it longer, not because I'm better.

Malcolm Gladwell's book *Outliers* talks about the 10,000-hour rule: mastery comes through time and

Chapter 6: Equipping the Saints

repetition. Even a person with average talent can become a master with 10,000 hours of practice. That just might be the case with me. After 35 plus years of preaching I just have a lot of reps, not necessarily a lot of talent.

No one was better at anything than Jesus—and yet, He entrusted the future of the Kingdom to twelve apostles. There was no Plan B. Equipping is not about excellence—it's about obedience to a bigger purpose.

> Now this is the testimony of John, when the Jews sent priests and Levites from Jerusalem to ask him, "Who are you?" He confessed, and did not deny, but confessed, "I am not the Christ." — *John 1:19-20 (NKJV)*

There was a time I tried to validate who I was through ministry. I was voted *least likely to succeed* in junior high. Girls rejected me. Then I found an anointing and a gift—and I started using it to prove I was somebody. Over time God revealed this to me and by His grace I have learned that ministry is not about me—it's about Him, and connecting the people He loves to Him. I am not the focus. I am just the conduit to help bring people to Jesus and Jesus to people. It was a very liberating day when I realized I am not Jesus!

Burnout happens when we try to be the Savior. I can't please everybody. Jesus was perfect and He couldn't please everybody. Some people will get mad and that's okay.

The Need to Feel Valuable

Sometimes people won't develop others because they feel more valuable when they are the only one on the team who can do a certain thing, or know a certain program, or are the only one with the key or passcodes, or the only one with the relationship with a specific person, etc. But this person's value is misplaced. The bottleneck on a team is not the most valuable player, but the person who refuses to develop others.

If our motive is to feel valuable, we become vulnerable to burnout.

In Leviticus 10, Aaron's sons offered *strange fire* before the Lord—and were burned up. When we feel burned *up*, burned *out*, or burned *by* ministry, we must look at this passage. In verse 3, the Lord says, "I will be glorified..." The implication is that the sons' *motive* wasn't to glorify the Lord—it was to glorify themselves.

Chapter 6: Equipping the Saints

- **MOTIVES**: When our motives aren't pure—and we want to be seen by people—we burn out in ministry.

- **METHODS**: Their fire didn't come from the altar of the Lord. It was 'strange fire,' not fire from the altar of the Lord. Only the fire that comes from the *altar of the Lord* keeps burning. Any fire not from the altar may start hot, but it won't last.

Many leaders begin in their own strength, as Moses did before his wilderness experience. Moses had a vision to deliver Israel—but he started in his own strength. When he saw an Egyptian beating a Hebrew, he killed the Egyptian. In that moment, he was essentially saying, **"Here I am."** But when his actions were exposed, he fled and spent 40 years in the wilderness as a shepherd. Then he encountered God at the burning bush.

> But Moses said to God, "Who *am* I that I should go to Pharaoh, and that I should bring the children of Israel out of Egypt?" – *Exodus 3:11 (NKJV)*

At first, Moses said, *"Here I am."* After 40 years, he asked, *"Who am I?"* That's the turning point. Because the real question isn't "Who am I?" but rather:

"Who is with us?" — *The Great I AM.*

Here is a Tweet-worthy statement: *God* can't be "I AM" until we know "We Are Not."

Similarly, Paul's transformation teaches us humility is essential for effective ministry. In *Acts 13:1*, Saul is sent on his first missionary journey. "Saul" means requested one—he was in demand. But God changed his name to Paul, which means little.

As Paul walked with Jesus, he became humbler:

- I am the least of the apostles. — *1 Corinthians 15:9 (NKJV)*

- To me, who am less than the least of all the saints, this grace was given... — *Ephesians 3:8 (NKJV)*

- That Christ Jesus came into the world to save sinners, of who I am the chief. — *1 Timothy 1:15 (NKJV)*

He went from being the man in demand to simply being "little." And in doing so, he became a vessel God could truly use.

Chapter 6: Equipping the Saints

The Fear of Being Replaced

Some don't develop and deploy others because they feel they will be replaced. Well, that is our job to work ourselves out of a job. The person who is good enough to work themselves out of a job will always have a job and a higher paying job because they are the most irreplaceable person on the team. The person most vulnerable to being replaced is the one who only does, rather than develops others.

To not replace yourself is to replace the wrong thing in your culture.

1 John 2:18 warns us that in the last days, the Antichrist will come. The word *anti* doesn't just mean "against"; it also means "in place of." In *Revelation 6*, we see that wars and famines follow. Whenever we put anything *in place of Christ*, the result is always destruction—famines and wars. Likewise, when we put ourselves in a role that we're unwilling to share or hand off, we are subtly putting ourselves *in place of* others, even of Christ's body functioning as it should.

> After these things the Lord appointed seventy others also, and sent them two by two before His face into every city and place where He Himself was about to go... — *Luke 10:1 (NKJV)*

The number 70 in Scripture symbolizes *everyone*. In Exodus, 70 people from Jacob's family entered Egypt to form a nation. In Genesis 10, 70 nations represent the Gentile world. So, when Jesus sent the 70, He was giving a picture of what it means to mobilize *everyone* for ministry.

> Then the seventy returned with joy... — *Luke 10:17 (NKJV)*

There is deep joy in being *sent* and in being *used* by God.

> For as we have many members in one body, but all the members do not have the same function, so we, *being* many, are one body in Christ, and individually members of one another. Having then gifts differing according to the grace that is given to us, *let us use them*... — *Romans 12:4–6 (NKJV)*

Growth in the Body happens when the members *use their gifts*. When people are equipped and empowered, the whole Church matures—and we begin to experience the joy of fruitfulness. We often use the word *volunteer*, but members of your body don't "volunteer." Your kidney doesn't take Sundays off. Your lungs don't sign up when it's convenient. You don't want volunteers—you want functioning members.

Chapter 6: Equipping the Saints

A funny but fitting example: there was once a TV interview with several bodybuilders. One of them, extremely muscular, was asked by the host, "What do you use those muscles for?" The man responded by flexing and posing to wild applause. The host asked again, "That's impressive, but what do you *use* them for?" The man posed again, smiling—but gave no answer. He had built muscles only to show them off—not to do anything with them.

So, ask yourself: Why are you building spiritual muscles? Why do you read your Bible, go to church, attend small group, or memorize Scripture? Is it just to show off your "Bible biceps," your "prayer pectorals," or your "glory glutes"? Or are you training for a purpose—*for the work of the ministry*? We were created for good works, and we build our muscles for work, the work of the ministry.

Equip Your Team

We have been talking about team, but you may be thinking I don't have anyone to EQUIP. Well, that is where you recruit someone. But we don't have budget to hire someone. Great! You have the gift of not enough. Sometimes churches with too much budget hire people for tasks that should be done by volunteers. Often, it's out of laziness or simply because it seems easier to pay some people to do it than to do our "job" of equipping saints for ministry.

Jesus didn't hire a staff, he recruited volunteers.

> Then He said to them, "Follow Me, and I will make you fishers of men." They immediately left *their* nets and followed Him. — *Matthew 4:19-20 (NKJV)*

Draft Your Team

Jesus didn't recruit volunteers—He voluntold draftees (He called them with authority to follow). A modern-day version might look like the IMF (Impossible Missions Force referenced in the *Mission: Impossible* movies) recruiter:

"What are you doing?"

"Nothing."

"Good—follow me."

They dropped what was in their hands to follow what was in a leader's heart.

Draft Your Team with Vision

What's in your heart must be bigger than what's in their hand. When you recruit, don't recruit to fill a gap, recruit to ignite a fire. Why? *"Set yourself on fire and people will come to watch you burn."*

Pay Them Well

We've *never* had enough money—and that's a gift—not enough. The gift of not enough forces us to do what is our calling and that is to equip the saints for the work of the ministry rather than just hiring more staff to do the ministry.

Think about Peter going home to explain his new role to his wife. There was no contract, no discussion of pay or benefits, no vacation days, no PTO, no 401k plans, etc. I wouldn't be surprised if Peter's wife had him sleep on the couch that first night after saying quitting his lucrative fishing business to follow a homeless Rabbi from Galilee.

The Offer Jesus Gave Wasn't a Salary—It Was a Cause and a Commission.

- **A Cause:** "You are my cause. I'm going to change you and make you."

- **A Commission:** "We're going to change the world together—fishers of men."

Money may buy success, but it doesn't buy significance. Success is what you do for yourself. Significance is what you do for others. "You can do something bigger *with us* than you ever could *without us*."

Rule: What you keep visible, you keep valuable. Start meetings with stories, not statistics. Celebrate what matters. People will rise to the level of what you *consistently honor* and *intentionally develop*.

Three Levels of Equipping: Heart, Head, Hands

We have been looking at **equipping**—now let's talk about **where** and **what** we are to equip in our team members. I love this verse about David:

> He also chose David His servant, and took him from the sheepfolds;... So he shepherded them according to the integrity of his heart, And guided them by the skillfulness of his hands. — *Psalm 78:70-72 (NKJV)*

There are three levels of someone we must develop.

Heart

God won't promote us beyond what our character can sustain.

> Keep your heart with all diligence, for out of it *spring* the issues of life. — *Proverbs 4:23 (NKJV)*

Head

God won't promote us beyond what our ability can manage. Jesus in the parable of the talents said this...

> And to one he gave five talents, to another two, and to another one, to each according to his own ability..."— *Matthew 25:15 (NKJV)*

Notice that one's ability was what determined what God could entrust them with.

Hands

God won't promote us beyond what our hands can hold.

Here are some resource recommendations for your team:

- Books (My favorite Leadership book is "The Road Less Stupid" by Keith Cunningham.)

- 360° reviews

- IDPs (Individual Development Plans)

- Coaching with an outside certified professional

- My free *All-Out Leadership* podcast – can be found on http://www.eriklawson.com/ and Spotify

When I'm coaching a team member, I approach it like a doctor: I don't want to treat only the symptom but the root cause. So, I ask myself, *Is this a heart issue, a head issue, or a hands issue?* We are very grace-filled with head and hands issues—we can teach skills and provide resources. Heart issues are different. I can't change someone's heart. Here at Element, the #1 cause of turnover is heart-related more than head or hands.

Equip the heart first, then the head, and finally the hands—and the whole body will grow strong.

Equipping the saints isn't optional—it's essential for a thriving, multiplying church. When leaders step back and empower others, God's work advances exponentially. Your role is not to do it all, but to develop and release others to do the work God has called them to. Let's commit to this holy partnership.

Chapter 7: Next — What Is Next

Next - *We celebrate today while seizing tomorrow.*

Success can be a double-edged sword. While we celebrate our wins, if we are not careful, they can lull us into complacency, blinding us to the need for continual growth and change. This chapter explores why 'today's success is the greatest enemy of tomorrow's success,' why change is essential, what often holds us back, and how to embrace change for lasting fruitfulness.

Today's Success Is the Greatest Enemy of Tomorrow's Success

Of the 58 Super Bowls since 1967 only 8 NFL teams have won back-to-back championships (the Steelers did it twice). Since the first MLB World Series in 1903, only 14 teams have won two in a row across 121 years.

The Element Way: Serving, Leading, and Building Teams

What does history teach us?

Success feels good, but it can deceive us into thinking the work is done. This complacency can stall growth and lead to decline. To thrive, we must keep moving forward. Today's success can be the greatest threat to tomorrow's success.

Sun Tzu, in *The Art of War*, wrote:

"Complacency is a silent adversary that can lead to errors and oversights."

#1 We Slowly Stop Doing the Things That Brought Success

We've heard the statement: *What got you here won't get you there.* **True!** But—if you stop doing what got you here, you won't *stay* here either. Success is built on the foundation of what got you here. The next level is simply the next brick. We see this in books like Jim Collins' *Good to Great* and *How the Mighty Fall*.

Examples from Everyday Life:

- We hit a spiritual high – then stop morning devotions, skip prayer.

Chapter 7: Next — What Is Next?

- Our marriage hits an anniversary milestone – then we stop dating our spouse, forget the flowers, and give them leftover time.

- We reach a fitness goal – then grab the donut, skip the gym, fall back into old habits.

- We hit a sales target – then stop making calls and neglect the follow-up.

- Our personal finances are finally in order – then we stop budgeting and slide back into debt.

The Bible reminds us again and again to 'press on' and remain connected to Christ, our source of life and growth *(John 15; Philippians 3:12).* This ongoing transformation is vital if we want to avoid stagnation.

> Abide in Me, and I in you. As the branch cannot bear fruit of itself, unless it abides in the vine, neither can you, unless you abide in Me. — *John 15:4 (NKJV)*

> Not that I have already attained, or am already perfected; but I press on, that I may lay hold of that for which Christ Jesus has

also laid hold of me. — *Philippians 3:12 (NKJV)*

Celebrate today — yes. But don't camp there. Keep pressing, keep on going.

#2 When we stop growing, we stand still, but progress keeps moving forward.

It would be like getting on the train called success. I get off at this stop because I arrived at my destination. Life is good. But then the train keeps going and I am left behind. We see this as people get older. They reach a level of fashion success. Then get off the train and stay in that same era of fashion. The problem is the fashion train keeps going. It's why we see old guys at Disney World that look like fashion train wreaks from 1984.

Back in 1996, during my youth ministry days, someone came up to me and said:

"Erik, your preaching is great... but I just can't get past your hair."

At the time, I still had a 1986 hairstyle — looked great, by the way! But he gently said,

"Let me take you to a stylist and help you out."

Chapter 7: Next — What Is Next?

I didn't like it at first. But I went through with it anyway. The following Wednesday, I walked into youth group with a new look. And the response?

"WOW, what happened to you? You look good!"

And you know what happened next? The kids started listening.

Changing my hairstyle wasn't just about appearance—it symbolized my willingness to grow and be relevant to those I served. Complacency can look like holding on to old habits that no longer serve our mission.

> But the Lord said to Samuel, "Do not look at his appearance or at his physical stature, because I have refused him. For *the Lord* does not see as man sees; for man looks at the outward appearance, but the Lord looks at the heart." — *1 Samuel 16:7-8 (NKJV)*

Some people quote this verse as an excuse not to grow, "God looks at the heart." True, but we are trying to reach man. How did the verse begin? "Man looks at the outward appearance." Some people can't get past the mess the messenger created to hear the message. Paul said, "I have become all things to all *men,* that I might by all means save some. Now this I do for the gospel's sake…." — *(1 Cor. 9:22b-23 NKJV)*

Some estimates say human knowledge is doubling every 12-months.

In the job market, today's skills become obsolete tomorrow. According to a 2023 Forbes article that due to AI, executives estimate that nearly half (49%) of the skills that exist in their workforce today won't be relevant in 2025. The same number, 47%, believe their workforces are unprepared for the future workplace.

I have seen this with Church over 35-yesars of ministry now. Churches were in their prime. God was moving. People were getting saved but then it stopped. They stay the same. Facilities stay the same. Worship songs stay the same. Styles stay the same. Methods of ministry remain the same. Slowly they dwindle and die. If we stop growing, we begin to die.

GOD'S WORD NEVER CHANGES! GOD'S TRUTH NEVER CHANGES! BUT we must change as leaders, Christ followers, parents, spouses, and methods must change because we live in a world that is ever changing. Never forget the message is sacred but not the methods of delivery. I am sure glad we are not still using Pony Express for mail delivery. Aren't you?

> But we all, with unveiled face, beholding as in a mirror the glory of the Lord, are being transformed into the same image from glory to glory, just as by the Spirit of the Lord. — *2 Corinthians 3:18 (NKJV)*

> Not that I have already attained, or am already perfected; but I press on, that I may lay hold of that for which Christ Jesus has also laid hold of me... — *Philippians 3:12 (NKJV)*

Four Reasons We Resist Change

As a church we must continually change. As Christians we must continually change. God established change as a constant from the beginning.

> "While the earth remains, Seedtime and harvest, Cold and heat, Winter and summer, And day and night Shall not cease." — *Genesis 8:22 (NKJV)*

From the beginning God established change as a part of life.

> To everything *there is* a season, A time for every purpose under heaven: A time to be born, And a time to die; A time to plant, And a time to pluck *what is* planted.
> — Ecclesiastes 3:1–2 (NKJV)

The heart of Christianity is change. The new birth is about the ultimate change. We go from glory to glory. The steps of a righteous man are ordered of the Lord. Human nature isn't comfortable with change. We are by nature creatures of habit.

#1 For some, change isn't comfortable

I heard one person say the only thing that likes change is a baby with dirty diapers. Some prefer the familiar of "The good old days," to the "unfamiliar of today." We love to compare today to yesterday. If we aren't careful, we will forget what "the good old days" were really like.

In 1902, the average life expectancy was 47. Only 14% of homes had a bathtub. Only 8% of homes had a telephone. A three-minute call from New York to Denver was $11 in 1902 currency. There were only 8,000 cars in the US and only 144 miles of paved roads. The maximum speed was 10mph. The average wage was 22 cents an hour. (You'd have to save up to shop at dollar store.)

Chapter 7: Next — What Is Next?

Change is constant—from technology to lifestyle — and resisting it means falling behind. Because comfort tempts us to cling to 'the good old days,' we stop innovating and risk decline.

Moses encountered this mentality while trying to bring Israel out of slavery from Egypt and to the Promise Land. A group was rebelling against Moses, and they had forgotten how bad the 'good old days' were.

> And Moses sent to call Dathan and Abiram the sons of Eliab, but they said, "We will not come up! *Is it* a small thing that you have brought us up out of a land flowing with milk and honey, to kill us in the wilderness, that you should keep acting like a prince over us? Moreover you have not brought us into a land flowing with milk and honey, nor given us inheritance of fields and vineyards." — *Numbers 16:12–14 (NKJV)*

How fast did they forget the cracking of the Egyptian taskmasters' whips and the life of slavery. They called Egypt, "a land flowing with milk and honey" which was not true. It was a land flowing with the blood, sweat, and tears of Israel under the burden of slavery. Their unbelief and glamorizing the 'good old days' kept them from entering the

Promise of God's best. Let's learn from their mistake and not repeat it!

#2 For some change brings a fear of the unknown

History has shown people resist new inventions/innovations because of fear. Many things we take for granted today were fought against with strong opposition in their beginning.

Human nature is to fear the unknown and criticize the thing we fear. I think it is funny how people will throw in statements like *"The Almighty never intended..."* Well, do you have a Bible verse to back that up? People criticize what they fear and try to validate it by tossing in "The Almighty..." If it is in the Bible, then fine. But if not, don't bring the Bible into it. Just admit it is your opinion.

Fear of the unknown keeps us stuck, even when our current path no longer works.

#3 For others, change brings the fear of learning the unknown

The philosopher Aristotle said the heavier an object the faster it will fall to earth. His theory went unchallenged for nearly 2,000 years. Galileo took a group of learned professors to the base of the leaning tower of Pisa and dropped a 10-pound and a one-pound weight at the same time. According to the Aristotle's theory the 10-pound weight should have landed first. However, both landed at the same time. In spite of the evidence, the so-called learned scholars refused to believe it.

We pick on doubting Thomas for his "unless I see and touch..." attitude he wouldn't believe it. Some people, even when they see it and touch it, would still refuse to believe.

Later Galileo, when proving Copernicus' theory that the earth was not the center of the universe, but that planets revolved around the sun, was thrown into prison and spent the rest of his life under house arrest. Some people would rather silence the voice of change than to change.

#4 For some, change brings a fear of failure

No one loves failure. But when we change our view of failure, we can experience new heights. Nothing great was ever achieved without the risk of failure. To get what you have never had you have to do what you've never done, and you can't do that without making some mistakes.

I like what Robert Kiyosaki, author of *Rich Dad Poor Dad* wrote about regarding the Texans' attitude about failure. In reference to the Alamo, and it's military failure, and in spite of their courageous stand. Rather than Texans holding their head in shame they turned it into a battle cry "Remember the Alamo." Then they turned it into a tourist's attraction. Gotta love Texans!

One constant in this world is change. I like what one man said, "Change is inevitable except from a vending machine." Henry Kissinger said, "For any student of history change is the law of life..."

Despite these natural resistances, change is necessary — here's why and how we must embrace it.

Why We Need Change?

Change will move us from negative to positive.

A native tribe in South America had been dying prematurely from strange unknown reasons for generations. It was finally discovered it was caused by the bite of an insect, which lived in the walls of their adobe homes. They had several possible solutions:

Chapter 7: Next — What Is Next?

- Destroy insects with insecticide
- Destroy and rebuild homes
- Move to another area
- They choose the 4th option which was to stay and do nothing about it

You may remember the old ABC's Wide World of Sports TV opening.

Spanning the globe to bring you the constant variety of sport! The thrill of victory. And the agony of defeat…

When they said "the agony of defeat" they flashed to a downhill skier crashing off the ski slopes with a horrific crash. Years later I read that the crash was deliberate by the skier, and he walked away with nothing more than a headache. He was gaining so much speed for his jump that he thought he would overshoot the landing, which would almost certainly be death. So, he made a split-second decision to avoid disaster. Many people are speeding towards disaster but rather than change course they just keep speeding ahead. They would rather complain about the collision than change course.

> But his wife looked back behind him, and she became a pillar of salt. — *Genesis 19:26 (NKJV)*

Jewish Historian Josephus claims to have seen the actual pillar of salt that was once Lots wife. If you choose to look back in life rather than forward, you turn into a pillar. A pillar goes nowhere. In life, one either progresses or regresses.

When Do We Create Change?

> "I am the true vine, and My Father is the vinedresser. Every branch in Me that does not bear fruit He takes away; and every *branch* that bears fruit He prunes, that it may bear more fruit."— *John 15:1-2 (NKJV)*

#1 When something is no longer fruitful.

What used to work no longer does. Outgrew its purpose. John Maxwell tells a story in his book *Developing the Leader Within You*, that I love. For no apparent reason an attendant stood at the foot of the stairway leading to the British House of Commons. This position was held in the attendant's family for three generations over the last 20 years. Someone checked to see how this position originated and found that the attendant's grandfather was placed there after the stairs had been painted to warn him or her of wet paint. The paint dried up, but the job didn't.

Chapter 7: Next — What Is Next?

#2 When the old traditions stand in the way of new progress.

> He answered and said to them, "Why do you also transgress the commandment of God because of your tradition?"— *Matthew 15:3 (NKJV)*

We have many great traditions. What we must be careful of is that we don't allow tradition to keep us from developing new traditions that come from needed change. When you look at many traditions in church today, they started out as good things to meet specific needs.

Sunday Night Service

Early in our church history most American churches were in rural farm countries. Before the automobile it would be a big ordeal to get the whole family to church. It wasn't practical to have mid-week services when distance and farming was a big factor. So why not have a potluck after church and have a Sunday night service too? Well, today transportation has solved much of that issue. Sunday night is not a New Testament commandment, but it is a church tradition. If a church chooses to have Sunday night service that is their prerogative but don't judge another church that choose not to.

Steeples

Were placed on churches so it could be more visible in the community. Church acted as a multipurpose civic facility as well a place of worship. You don't see any steeple in the early New Testament church because it was created to meet a need for a different and later era.

Chairs on Platform

I am not sure as to what their origin, but I am sure it was meeting a need of the time. Again, not a New Testament commandment but a church tradition. Personally, I am not of fan of this because I want the focus on the communication and not those sitting on the platform. I also would be a distraction if I was sitting on the platform because I struggle to sit still.

Pews

Were an affordable way to seat a larger number of people. Churches in rural communities didn't have the budgets of many of the churches today and due to the manufacturing industry, chairs were much more expensive. Pews meet a specific need to seat the most amount of people for the best price. But it is not a New Testament commandment.

We must remember why the tradition/policy/procedure was created in the first place. It was created to serve people. When it no longer serves and stands in the way of serving others better, we need change. We love people, not policy. We love people, not programs.

> And He said to them, "The Sabbath was made for man, and not man for the Sabbath." — *Mark 2:27 (NKJV)*

#3 When the return on investment is too low? ROI

There are times a good idea is no longer sustainable when you look at how much investment of resources it takes. Return On Investment (ROI).

When I was Associate Youth Pastor (eventually I became the Senior Youth Pastor) at Oneighty© the youth ministry of Church On The Move in Tulsa, Oklahoma, we wanted to create a way to follow up with visitors. I was given the ministry and asked to develop a way to follow up. I asked myself if a visitor comes to our youth ministry why wouldn't they want to come back? Well, the services were good, the facilities were great. It came down to that it was too big and impersonal.

So, let's visit them. But what teen wants a visit from someone they don't know. Especially an old person. Well, why don't we visit them and just leave them a sign? Pretty cool. Next, I had to figure how who I needed to recruit for such a ministry. So, I asked myself, "What kind of teen would want to run around in the middle of the night putting signs in people's yards?" That's easy, the same one that keeps putting toilet paper in my trees every Friday night. What do they look like? I don't know, I have never seen them. Must be wearing camouflage. So, we designed a program called IMF (Impossible Mission Force) to follow up with visitors. We built it like a SPEC Ops team. We had military ranks, uniforms, and a private room with a keypad entry that only IMF Agents got the code. Even the janitor didn't have the room code. We had IMF in the floor title like the CIA headquarters. It was so cool. Needless to say, it attracted lots of outlier students into ministry who would have never made it on the greeter team. They got a chance to be used by God and make a difference in many lives. It was great until we started running 1,000 teens. It outgrew our ability for our size. So, what do we do? We had to quit and change that ministry and move on to the next thing. And you know the next thing was never as cool, but it was effective, so visitors didn't fall through the cracks—and that is what matters most.

Chapter 7: Next — What Is Next?

What Never Changes?

While much must change, three things remain constant: God's character, His Word, and the Church's mission. These are our anchor as we adapt.

- **The Lord** – The same yesterday, today, and forever.

- **The Word** – Thy word is truth – God's word is the North Star – the never moving compass we use to navigate our life. People will be offended by the gospel, but we will never change the gospel to be non-offensive. We change the methods but not the message.

- **The purpose of the church** - Love God, Love People

How To Change It?

When you see the need for change in your life what do you do? Where do you start?

#1 Stop

You have heard the saying "when the horse is dead, dismount." Some people would rather stay on a dead horse than dismount. Top strategies for dealing with a dead horse:

- Buy a stronger whip

- Change riders

- Appoint a committee to study the dead horse

- Send out a memo declaring the horse isn't really dead

- Hire an expensive consultant to find "the real problem."

- Harness several dead horses together for increased speed and efficiency

- Rewrite the standard definition of live horse

Definition of insanity is doing what you've always done but expecting different results. Stop and dismount from the unproductive activity in your life.

#2 Start

The greatest way to change our circumstances is to change ourselves. D.L. Moody "I've had more trouble with D.L Moody than any other man alive."

Television host Jack Paar "looking back, my life seems like one long obstacles race with me as its chief obstacle."

To change the world, start by changing yourself. Let's quit pointing the finger at others and start taking ownership for what we can change and ourselves. I am not accountable for others, but I am accountable for what I can change and for myself.

#3 Steps

> And the Lord your God will drive out those nations before you little by little; you will be unable to destroy them at once, lest the beasts of the field become *too* numerous for you. But the Lord your God will deliver them over to you and will inflict defeat upon them until they are destroyed. — *Deuteronomy 7:22-23 (NKJV)*

God doesn't give us success all at once because it would overtake us. He gives us success little by little as we are ready to handle the next level. New level, new devil. Gordon Sullivan, Former Army Chief of Staff said, "For an enduring organization, there is no finite end state only a journey—always becoming and never being."

God calls us to a journey of constant growth—from glory to glory. While His Word and purpose remain firm, our methods and hearts must remain flexible and humble. Let's commit to celebrating our victories without settling, embracing change without fear, and pressing on in faith, trusting that God will guide us into what's next.

Chapter 8: Speaking Truth with Grace

Truth - *We are graciously candid with ourselves and others.*

In every real relationship—family, team, or church—conflict is inevitable. Maybe you've heard the old Wendy's commercial slogan, "Where's the beef?" The commercial questioned whether a burger had real substance, we must ask—does our boldness carry biblical truth, or is it just personal frustration dressed as righteousness? Well, when you do life closely with people, the "beef" will eventually show up—misunderstandings, hurt feelings, or unmet expectations. The question isn't *if* you are going to have a "beef" with someone, but *how* will you serve it when it comes? Some are serving it a little too "raw." Hopefully this next chapter will equip us to serve the "beef" flavored with a little more "well done" good and faithful servant.

Many Christians mistakenly believe that anger or confrontation is ungodly. But Scripture doesn't tell us never to get angry—it says, "Be angry, and do not sin." *(Eph. 4:26 NKJV)* God gave us emotions, including anger, to act as internal indicators—not dictators. When guided by truth and delivered with love, even hard conversations can become holy ground.

In this chapter, we explore how to *speak the truth in love*—the way Jesus did: never compromising truth, never withholding grace.

Be Angry, And Do Not Sin

God Created Us With Our Emotions

Some people are trying to remove emotions from their Christianity. God didn't create us to be emotionless zombies. Emotions are given from God to enhance our life experience. The whole Bible is packed with emotion. Have you read the Psalms? Every emotion imaginable is inside the book of Psalms. Life is emotion! Take out emotion and you take out life.

Anger is an emotion that acts as a protective mechanism. It can be a motivator for good. A righteous anger has motivated many leaders to rise up and bring about change. Righteous anger inspired:

- David to kill a giant.
- Martin Luther to cause a reformation of the church.
- Pilgrims to leave Europe and settle a new nation to worship God freely.
- William Wilberforce to fight to end slavery in England.
- Our founding Fathers to cast off the chains of dictatorship and form a new nation.

Anger is like electricity—powerful and potentially dangerous. When harnessed well, it can be useful. When misused, it can be destructive. Anger is the same way.

The question isn't will you have a beef with someone, the question is when it happens, how are you going to serve it?

Speak The Truth In Love

Before we can speak the truth, we must first understand what truth is. In *John 17:17 NKJV*, Jesus says, "Sanctify them by Your truth. Your word is truth." Truth is not subjective opinion—it is rooted in God's Word and His unchanging character.

Jesus is described in *John 1:14 NKJV* as being "full of grace and truth." Likewise, *Ephesians 4:15 NKJV* exhorts us to "speak the truth in love." In both

Ephesians and John, we see that truth must be paired with love and grace—it's not an optional combination. Truth without love becomes harsh, and love without truth becomes hollow. Jesus modeled both perfectly.

When we confront sin or error, we're not called to win arguments—we're called to win hearts. Speaking truth in love means we care more about the person's restoration than our need to be right.

> Therefore, putting away lying, "Let each one of *you* speak truth with his neighbor," for we are members of one another. "Be angry, and do not sin": do not let the sun go down on your wrath, nor give place to the devil. — *Ephesians 4:25-27 (NKJV)*

We are to speak the truth in love. What does that mean? Jesus is the perfect model in everything. Love and truth are like a warm fireplace on a cold winter's night. They provide both light and heat.

- Truth without love is like the light of a fire without warmth.
- Love without truth is like the warmth of the fire without light.
- Truth without love makes people cold in the light.

Chapter 8: Speaking Truth with Grace

- Love without truth makes people stumble in the dark.

We need both truth and love. Interesting that Apostle John writes about love more than any New Testament writer but also uses the word truth more than any writer. He uses the word Truth in the Gospel of John twenty times, nine times in 1 John, five times in 2 John, and 5 more times in 3 John. We must speak the truth in love.

> And the Word became flesh and dwelt among us…full of grace and truth. — *John 1:14 (NKJV)*

First Jesus starts with grace. He is full of grace. Not half full. Not running on empty. We see two clear examples of Jesus coming in grace and truth. First, when he corrects the seven Churches in Rev. 2-3, He starts with whatever good He can find. He speaks grace. Then he corrects five of the seven with truth. Looking at Jesus' word to the church of Ephesus and Thyatira we see one strong in truth and weak in grace and the other is weak in grace but strong in truth. He corrects both churches. Ephesus was weak in its love yet faithful to judge false teachers. They had truth but lost love. Thyatira was growing in their love but was too tolerant of false teachers. Thyatira had "love" but lost truth.

To the woman caught in adultery in John chapter eight Jesus first draws attention to those holding rocks ready to stone this woman that they were also guilty and had no right to throw rocks. Next, we see him ask her, "Where are thy accusers? Who has condemned you?" After they had all left, she says, "No One Lord." He replies, "Neither do I condemn you." That's grace.

Then He follows it with truth, "Go and sin no more." He started with grace then gave truth. I accept you as a person, but this behavior is not acceptable. It's sin. But I am enabling you through my Word to be free to go and sin no more.

Notice Ephesians says, "Speak the TRUTH in love." What is truth? God's word is truth. There is a difference between your opinion and Gods Truth. They are not always in alignment.

I have had many people use this verse to say some very harsh things to me over the years. "Just speaking the truth in love pastor." Well, the truth was that 95% of the time it was their opinion not an actual BIBLICAL truth they could back up with scripture. Rupertus Meldenius, a 17th-century Lutheran theologian, is best attributed to promoting the philosophy:

- In essential beliefs – we believe there should be unity
- In non-essential beliefs – we believe there should be liberty (Romans 14)
- In all our beliefs – we believe that there must be love toward each other

HOW to Speak the Truth in Love?

We are looking at truth and speaking the truth in love. However, there are a few Bible verses we should look at before we move into HOW to speak the truth in love.

> A person's wisdom yields patience; it is to one's glory to overlook an offense. — *Proverbs 19:11 (New International Version NIV)*

> And above all things have fervent love for one another, for "love will cover a multitude of sins." — *1 Peter 4:8 (NKJV)*

Before we speak truth in love, we should ask is this something worth speaking about? Some problems are worth ignoring.

Greek Philosopher Publius said, "I have often regretted my speech, but never my silence."

> In the multitude of words sin is not lacking,
> But he who restrains his lips *is* wise. —
> *Proverbs 10:19 (NKJV)*

Here are five questions I ask myself before speaking.

(Most of the time – I don't get an A+ on this one but I am getting better):

- **Is this just a misunderstanding?**
  I try to give the benefit of the doubt when this is contrary to what I know of that person's character.

- **If this continues, will this hurt our relationship?**
  Don't make mountains out of molehills.

- **Is this a battle worth fighting?**
  Is this going to change anything?

There are times when confrontation is necessary. And at times to keep unity it should be overlooked.

> So the Lord scattered them abroad from there over the face of all the earth, and they ceased building the city. — *Genesis 11:8 (NKJV)*

Chapter 8: Speaking Truth with Grace

> The language of the cross and the Holy Spirit brought everyone together. — *Acts 2 (NKJV)*

There can only be true unity through the cross. I would rather be divided by a truth than united by a lie.

- **Is this even my battle?**
  Don't take up an offense for someone else.

  > He who passes by *and* meddles in a quarrel not his own is *like* one who takes a dog by the ears. — *Proverbs 26:17 (NKJV)*

  Taking a dog by the ears is a sure way to get bit. I have found when I jump into other people's quarrels it comes back to bite me.

- **Is this an opinion or a fact that I am upset about?**

  As we established earlier, truth isn't about personal feelings—it's about alignment with God's Word.

Necessary Confrontation

Let's look at what to do when we need to confront someone.

> Tremble and do not sin; when you are on your beds, search your heart and be silent.
> — *Psalms 4:4 (NIV)*

We are told to do three things when we are angry:

- Step back

- Search your heart

- Be silent

We can see Jesus apply this in his ministry. When Jesus overturned tables in the temple *(Matthew 21:12-13 NKJV)*, He wasn't being 'mean'—He was confronting what others avoided. In the same way, confronting sin today may feel uncomfortable, but it honors truth and protects spiritual health. When people hear of him driving out the money changers, they think Jesus just reacted in a fit of rage off the cuff.

> Jesus entered Jerusalem and went to the temple courts. He looked around at everything, but since it was already late, he went out to Bethany with the Twelve. — Mark 11:11 (NIV)

> Now the next day…they came to Jerusalem. Then Jesus went into the temple and began to drive out those who bought and sold in the temple…. — Mark 11:12b, 15 (NKJV)

Jesus surveyed the situation. Stepped back, slept on it, and then determined the appropriate way to confront this situation. While you are thinking about what to say, here is a helpful ACRYNOM: THINK.

#1 T – Is it Truthful?

> but, speaking the truth in love, may grow up in all things into Him who is the head—Christ. — Ephesians 4:15 (NKJV)

One time a man asked me: *"Pastor, do you even pray when you are writing your sermons? I get nothing out of your preaching."* Well, it was his truth, based on a feeling, but not the truth. The truth was he was offended at something else, and it turned off his ability to hear the truth through my preaching. Look at the word offend, it is "OFF END." When we allow our hearts to be offended it leads to ministry turning off and it comes to an end in one way or another. Even with understanding that, they were very painful words he spoke to me. They cut deeply and it wasn't a Biblical truth—just his opinion. Interestingly enough, that morning, before this man's conversation with me, a lady who had been in our church for years said, that recently my preaching had been the best she had ever heard since being at Element and she was getting so much from it. Two people sitting in the same service at the same time but each in a totally different place spiritually. On another side note in the Parable of the sower, Jesus never said anything negative about the sower of the seed, the focus was the soil of the men's hearts. Some hearts were hard, crowded, and full of unbelief, but others were soft and fertile. Before you get critical of the Sower of the seed, check your soil of your heart.

#2 H – Is it Helpful? Or is it going to harm?

> Let no corrupt word proceed out of your mouth, but what is good for necessary edification, that it may impart grace to the hearers. — *Ephesians 4:29 (NKJV)*

Is it helpful? Can they do anything to change it? When I was younger and still growing, I had a lady say, *"your ears are lopsided."* Well, it was true but not helpful. What could I do about it? So, I was just self-conscious for years. Thank you very much.

#3 I – Is it Inspirational? Is it going to build up or tear down?

Does this build them up? Second, is it their needs or is it my need to speak or be right that motivates me? I have been guilty of the last much more than the first.

#4 N – Is it Necessary? Is this a battle worth fighting?

I lose many battles to win wars. You can only fight on so many battle fronts. When it comes to certain truths, we cannot compromise! *Sam 11* — An Ammonite (Ammonite is a picture of the flesh) named Nahash came against Jabesh-gilead (belonging to the half tribe of Manasseh) to attack it. Nahash means, "serpent." He would make a peace treaty with them if they would put out their right eye. The Ammonites' demand to gouge out Israel's eyes wasn't just violence—it was humiliation. Saul's bold rejection shows us that peace isn't worth the price of compromise. Today, we're often pressured to "get along" at the expense of truth and turn a "blind eye" but spiritual leadership means standing firm even when it's unpopular.

Satan wants us to turn a blind eye and to live with half-truths. Our culture has settled for a lot of half-truths. Jesus said, "We will know the truth and it will set us free." He didn't say you will know the half-truth and it will set you free. In fact, a half-truth is still a full lie!

#5 K – Is it Kind?

> A soft answer turns away wrath, But a harsh word stirs up anger. — *Proverbs 15:1 (NKJV)*

How To Confront?

"Moreover if your brother sins against you, go and tell him his fault between you and him alone. If he hears you, you have gained your brother. But if he will not hear, take with you one or two more, that 'by the mouth of two or three witnesses every word may be established.' And if he refuses to hear them, tell *it* to the church. But if he refuses even to hear the church, let him be to you like a heathen and a tax collector." — *Matthew 18:15–17 (NKJV)*

Chapter 8: Speaking Truth with Grace

Step 1: Do Go to the Offender

ITS DOES NOT SAY GO TO OTHER PEOPLE – By definition that is gossip.

> Lord, who may abide in Your tabernacle? Who may dwell in Your holy hill? He who walks uprightly, And works righteousness, And speaks the truth in his heart, who does not backbite with his tongue, …Nor does evil to his neighbor, nor does he take up a reproach against his friend; — *Psalm 15:1-3 (NKJV)*

This Psalm was written while David was returning the Ark from captivity by the Philistines. Hebrew word "taketh" literally means "receive." A righteous person doesn't receive gossip or slander about another person. To receive it is to be just as guilty as the one speaking it.

> Who *is* the man *who* desires life, And loves *many* days, that he may see good? Keep your tongue from evil, And your lips from speaking deceit. — *Psalm 34:12-13 (NKJV)*

You can't spew poison and not get poisoned yourself. You can't say the word gossssssssip and not sound like a serpent. Well, there is truth in what I am saying...The Bible also addresses the issue of false witness.

> "You shall not bear false witness against your neighbor." — *Exodus 20:16 (NKJV)*

The one time in the Gospels *(Matt. 26:59 NKJV)* that this phrase is used illustratively is when someone took the words of Jesus and twisted them against him. If it is the example of a false witness given, then only one is needed for an example. They gave a half-truth but in God's eyes it was still a full lie. Giving the right information for the wrong implication is still sin!

When we bear false witness, we are actual doing the work of Satan because he is the accuser of the brethren *(Rev. 12:10 NKJV)*. Jesus is our advocate. When we fail to say what Jesus says over our brethren, we are only giving half-truths. When we stand before God there is no reward for doing the work of Satan which is to tear the brethren down.

Chapter 8: Speaking Truth with Grace

#1 Timing

> A man has joy by the answer of his mouth, and a word *spoken* in due season, how good it is! — Proverbs 15:23 (NKJV)

> "I still have many things to say to you, but you cannot bear *them* now." — John 16:12 (NKJV)

Examples of bad timing:

- Right place – Not email or text, use a private setting, face-to-face.
- Right people - Not in front of people who are not part of this.
- Not before something big: My staff know not to hit me with something before I go on stage to preach.
- Not when you won't have time to finish it.
- Not when you are still fuming.

#2 Tact

In warfare rarely is a frontal assault the best tactic. The same is true in communication. Guerrilla warfare tactics tend to have much better outcomes. For example, when I need to confront someone and set a time to meet, I rarely announce the purpose of the conversation. If I did, they go into defense mode and begin preparing their defenses before we even meet.

> A brother offended is *harder to win* than a strong city, And contentions *are* like the bars of a castle. — *Proverbs 18:19 (NKJV)*

When we start the conversation, I begin with statement/questions like these, "Could we revisit such and such... Could I get your help with something... I could use some clarity on... I might be missing something. Could you help fill in the gaps..."

A great book to help sharpen you communication skill is *Fierce Conversations* by Susan Scott. It's not a Christian book and I wouldn't use all the methods she mentions but there are enough good things in it that it will help. Like one of my Bible College professors would always say, "Eat the hay and spit out the sticks."

#3 Tone

70-93% of communication is non-verbal. I can't hear what you said because the way you said it was too loud. This is often the biggest break down, because it's not what, but how, it was said.

#4 How To Give Feedback

- When you said/did...it made me feel...
- Help me understand
- Listen to understand
- Dialog for resolution
- Resolve the matter or agree to disagree
- Close the door on it or STEP #2

STEP 2: Do Go up if necessary

If you are on staff and run into a roadblock with your leadership. It's ok to go up.

Winston Churchill said "Criticism may not be agreeable, but it is necessary. It fills the same function as pain in the human body; it calls attention to an unhealthy state of things."

> Faithful *are* the wounds of a friend, But the kisses of an enemy *are* deceitful. — *Proverbs 27:6 (NKJV)*

> As iron sharpens iron, so one person sharpens another. — *Proverbs 27:17 (NIV)*

Everyone has blind spots, and God uses others to help us see those.

How To Receive Feedback

- Don't react – I want to get better – listen for a kernel of truth
- Listen to understand – this is hard because I want to regroup my defense
- What I hear you saying is...
- I can image that made you feel...empathy is a pillar of emotional intelligence
- I am sorry – own anything you can (meekness is strength under control)
- Clarify – Can I share what I meant or what I was intending? (there are always two sides)
- Thank you and invite them to do this again!

There are some people who can never be corrected.

> Even the brightest sun can't make a blind man see.

There are some who are blind by choice. In Matt. 13 Jesus explained this is why He spoke in parables. That seeing they may not see and hearing they may not hear. Those who wanted to see could but those who didn't want to could not see. They don't want to see; therefore they can't see the truth.

Chapter 8: Speaking Truth with Grace

Why Do We Avoid Conflict?

There are many reasons we avoid conflict so let's just touch on a few of the most common.

#1 Doesn't feeling loving or Christ like

People love to quote *Matt. 7:1* "Judge not..." but verse 15 later in *Matt. 7:15-16* says judge a tree by its fruit. The context of *7:1* is judge not unto condemnation and *7:15* is judgment for identification. It's our job as pastors and parents to warn of false doctrine and false teachers.

> "For whom the Lord loves He chastens, And scourges every son whom He receives." If you endure chastening, God deals with you as with sons; for what son is there whom a father does not chasten? But if you are without chastening, of which all have become partakers, then you are illegitimate and not sons. — *Hebrew 12:6-8 (NKJV)*

Jesus is love yet said some pretty direct things. Even harsh sounding things.

To Peter: "Get behind Me, Satan!" *(Matt. 16:23, NKJV)* Jesus wasn't calling Peter Satan himself, but rebuking the mindset influenced by the enemy.

About Herod: "Go, tell that fox…" (*Luke 13:32, NKJV*) In that culture, calling someone a *fox* implied being sly, crafty, or deceitful.

To the Pharisees: "You are like whitewashed tombs which indeed appear beautiful outwardly, but inside are full of dead *men's* bones and all uncleanness." *(Matthew 23:27, NKJV)* Jesus exposed their hypocrisy: outwardly religious, inwardly corrupt.

#2 Personality

Some personalities like sanguine or "I" on the DISC are more people oriented. Someone who is melancholier or "C" on the DISC tends to be more introverted. Both of these tendencies can make confrontation more challenging. However, Biblical communication and confrontation is a choice we make regardless of our personality bent. We can't let our natural personality leaning keep us from obeying scripture. My personality which is "high D" (more dominant and direct) can't become an excuse to not be loving and grace filled when communicating. Confrontation comes easier for me where grace and gentleness may come easier for some, but we are still all called to be accountable to scripture regardless of our personality bent. Someone else you may be naturally gracious BUT you have to work to confront. Personality doesn't excuse us from OBEYING GOD'S WORD.

#3 Fear of offending

> The fear of man brings a snare, But whoever trusts in the LORD shall be safe. — *Proverbs 29:25 (NKJV)*

I would rather offend you than God. If I fear God, I need not fear anything else.

#4 I don't want to cause trouble

Not dealing with it is what causes trouble. That's like letting cancer grow because you don't want to cause trouble. Communication helps remove the cancer before it metastasizes.

#5 I don't want to lose my job

No one has ever lost a job here at Element for healthy communication and confrontation. But if we don't deal with this stuff, it can disqualify us from the team. We have had to let some people go because they were unwilling to deal with issues, listen to other people's concerns, or dialogue for personal and professional growth.

#6 They are higher in authority than me

There are times people feel they can't speak up because someone is above them. In some cultures that may be true but at Element we believe healthy communication transcends flow charts. We see in both Paul and Peter's writings this truth:

> Submitting to one another in the fear of God. — *Ephesians 5:21 (NKJV)*

> Likewise you younger people, submit yourselves to *your* elders. Yes, all of *you* be submissive to one another, and be clothed with humility, for "God resists the proud, but gives grace to the humble." — *1 Peter 5:5 (NKJV)*

There are times it is appropriate to appeal to someone higher in authority, but what is just as important is how we do it—always with respect and humility.

> Do not rebuke an older man harshly, but exhort him as if he were your father. — *1 Timothy 5:1 (NIV)*

#7 Revenge – You are letting them fail

Chapter 8: Speaking Truth with Grace

I have seen some people let others fail because they were jealous or harbored unresolved bitterness toward them. That's not godly nor healthy for any team. That is like being on the football team and watching someone fumble the ball and just standing there watching. Even worse, what would you think of the teammate who saw the fumble and rejoiced about it?

Truth and love are not enemies. They are teammates. One gives us clarity; the other gives us compassion. Jesus embodied both—*full of grace and truth.* Speaking the truth in love is not a license to vent or a call to avoid confrontation—it is a sacred invitation to help each other grow in Christ.

Conflict isn't the enemy—*unresolved* conflict is. Let's be people who lean in, speak up, and do it with wisdom, humility, and courage. When we speak truth in love, we reflect Jesus—and we create a community where healing, growth, and unity are possible.

Chapter 9: Stewardship — Faithfully Managing Time, Talent, and Treasure

Stewardship - *We honor God when we faithfully treasure people, time, and money.*

Stewardship is more than just a responsibility—it's a sacred trust. Everything we have—our time, talents, and treasures—are gifts from God, entrusted to us to manage faithfully for His glory and the good of others. How we steward these resources reveals the condition of our hearts and our commitment to God's mission. In this chapter, we will explore the biblical foundation of stewardship, the importance of faithfulness in managing what God has given us, and practical ways to steward our time and resources wisely. As we learn to honor God through stewardship, we position ourselves to experience His blessings and fulfill our calling with greater purpose and impact.

> *For the kingdom of heaven is* like a man traveling to a far country, *who* called his own servants and delivered his goods to them. And to one he gave five talents, to another two, and to another one, to each according

to his own ability; and immediately he went on a journey. — *Matthew 25:14-15 (NKJV)*

The first two stewards doubled what they were given, but the third buried his talent. When the man returned from his journey, he called the stewards to give an account just as when Jesus returns, he will call us to give an account of all He has entrusted to our care.

So take the talent from him, and give *it* to him who has ten talents. "For to everyone who has, more will be given, and he will have abundance; but from him who does not have, even what he has will be taken away." — *Matthew 25:28-29 (NKJV)*

We learn several important truths from this passage.

Biblical Foundation of Stewardship

#1 God owns everything. I am just a steward.

Steward: "A person employed to manage another's property."

Chapter 9: Stewardship — Faithfully Managing Time, Talent, and Treasure

We get into all kinds of troubles when we think it's our time, our talent, our treasure, our life. Everything we have is from God, by God, and for God *(Col. 1:16)*. This should change the way I think about life. As a staff member or volunteer at Element we are stewards of God's Church and His resources.

#2 God is looking for increase

He rewarded the two stewards who turned what they had into more. He rebuked the steward who buried his talent. He didn't lose it. If Jesus rebuked the servant who did not lose his talent but buried it, what would He say to us who squander what we have, go into debt, and still ask for more?

#3 God doesn't compare us to others

He didn't say to the guy with two, "Why didn't you produce five more like that guy?" He saw that he doubled what he was given, just like the first steward. Jesus isn't comparing us to anyone else. He isn't holding us accountable for what he hasn't given us, but only what he has given us. In fact, that was part of the wrong thinking that the servant had who buried his talent.

> "I knew you to be a hard man, reaping where you have not sown, and gathering

> where you have not scattered seed." — *Matthew 25:24 (NKJV)*

In the Gospel of John, after Jesus restores Peter, Peter sees John and asks Jesus:

> Peter, seeing him, said to Jesus, "But Lord, what *about* this man?" Jesus said to him, "If I will that he remain till I come, what *is that* to you? You follow Me." — *John 21:21-22 (NKJV)*

Peter get your eyes off others and put them on me. Peter might have been reminded of a time he walked on water and then sank after a few steps. Why? He got his eyes off Jesus. You will always sink into depression and despair when you look at others. You can always find someone ahead of you, beside you, and behind you. Let's fix our eyes on Jesus. *(Heb. 12:2)*

Look at what happened next:

> Then this saying went out among the brethren that this disciple would not die. Yet Jesus did not say to him that he would not die, but "If I will that he remain till I come, what *is that* to you?" — *John 21:23 (NKJV)*

When you start trying to figure out someone else's calling or word from God, you almost always get it wrong. You aren't graced for their race. It only leads to rumors, and these are almost always wrong.

#4 God won't give us more that we can manage

> He who *is* faithful in what *is* least is faithful also in much; and he who is unjust in what *is* least is unjust also in much. Therefore if you have not been faithful in unrighteous mammon, who will commit to your trust the true *riches?* And if you have not been faithful in what is another man's, who will give you what is your own? — *Luke 16:10-12 (NKJV)*

If your kid can't ride a bicycle, would you give him your car to drive? If your kid doesn't take care of your clunker, would you give your nice car? No, you wouldn't. So why would God give us more when we haven't been faithful with what we have. If we want God to give us more (whatever that might be) we must first prove we are faithful with what we have.

Early in the church's life, I was complaining to God about how hard it was to lead our 300 people. I then proceeded to ask God to grow our church. His reply was, "If you can't handle the 300 how can you handle 1,000 or 3,000?"

"If you have run with the footmen, and they have wearied you, Then how can you contend with horses? And *if* in the land of peace, *In which* you trusted, *they wearied you*, Then how will you do in the floodplain of the Jordan?" — *Jeremiah 12:5 (NKJV)*

The Three Gifts: Time, Talents, Treasure

God has entrusted each of us with three precious gifts—time, talents, and treasure. These are the resources we are called to steward faithfully throughout our lives. They are not ours to hoard or waste but to manage wisely and generously, reflecting God's heart and purposes. In this section, we'll unpack each of these gifts, exploring what it means to honor God by investing our time well, using our unique talents to serve, and giving our treasure with a joyful and faithful heart. Understanding and embracing these gifts is key to living a life of stewardship that pleases God and advances His kingdom.

Time

From the moment we were conceived the clock started ticking. Someday the clock will run out. Game over. There is no reset button. Make it count!

Chapter 9: Stewardship — Faithfully Managing Time, Talent, and Treasure

I love the movie *Braveheart*. I just feel manly watching it. For me it's like walking into Home Depot. I just feel manly. I don't know how to use most of the tools, but I go in when I need a testosterone recharge. William Wallace said, "Death comes to us all." And "All men die but not all men really live!"

We all have the same amount of time each day, 24 hours or 1440 minutes or 86,400 seconds. We all have the same. No more and no less. But not all people get the same results with it.

For instance, let's look at Bill Gates, one of the wealthiest men in the world. If he were to see a $100 bill on the ground as he was walking it would be better for him not to pick it up. He would lose money in the amount of time it took for Him to bend down and pick up the bill. Most of us however would not only bend over but also take time out to do a little end zone shuffle. "Oh, ya it's my birthday." Bill Gates doesn't have more time than you and me but he probably manages his time a bit differently.

Jesus knew how to maximize his time. In 3.5 years, he changed the world. There have been more books written about him and more songs sung about him than any other person in history. All from three and a half years. John said of him all the books couldn't contain all the works he did.

> See then that you walk circumspectly, not as fools but as wise, redeeming the time, because the days are evil. — *Ephesians 5:15-16 (NKJV)*

> So teach *us* to number our days, That we may gain a heart of wisdom. — *Psalm 90:12 (NKJV)*

Successful people never "kill time." They never run down the clock. Time is the substance of life, therefore, to kill time is to kill life.

1. Time is more valuable than money

You can always get more money, but you can never get more time. Jesus said it this way:

> For what will it profit a man if he gains the whole world, and loses his own soul? Or what will a man give in exchange for his soul? — *Mark 8:36-37 (NKJV)*

18th Century Atheist French Philosopher Voltaire on his death bed reportedly was terrified because that morning he saw a vision of hell. The physician, waiting up with Voltaire at his death, said that he cried out with utter desperation, "I am abandoned by God and man. I will give you half of what I am

Chapter 9: Stewardship — Faithfully Managing Time, Talent, and Treasure

worth if you will give me six months of life. Then I shall go to hell, and you will go with me."

Contrast that with the first Christian to be killed for his faith, Stephen. As he was dying, while being stoned to death with rocks…

> "Look," he said, "I see heaven open and the Son of Man standing at the right hand of God." At this they covered their ears and, yelling at the top of their voices, they all rushed at him." — *Acts 7:56-57 (NIV)*

All other New Testament references to Jesus is that He is seated at the right hand of God the Father. Why was he standing. I believe Jesus was giving Him a standing OVATION for a race well run. Evangelist D. L. Moody, on his deathbed, said, "I see Earth receding and heaven is opening. God is calling me."

I love this statement written by someone at the end of their life. "First, I was dying to finish high school and start college. And then I was dying to finish college and start working. And then I was dying to marry and have children. And then I was dying for my children to grow old enough for school so I could return to work. And then I was dying to retire. And now I am dying and suddenly I realized I forgot to live." We have been given one life this side of heaven. Let's make it count!

2. Goal setting

We are looking at the value of time and how to get the most from it. To win with your time you must define the end zone. What and where is the goal?

Too many people are playing football like a man named Roy Riegels. In 1929, Roy Riegels went into the Rose Bowl as the center and captain of California's football team against Georgia Tech. In the second quarter he picked up a fumble from Georgia Tech and started towards the end zone. He had gotten hit and lost his bearing and started running again, but the wrong way. He ran all the way to the first yard line of his own team's end zone before he was stopped by his own team. His error cost his team two points and the game, and he had to live the rest of his life with the name "Wrong Way Reigels."

Running the wrong way in a game is costly, but many people spend their entire lives running in circles or in the wrong direction. We were created by God to win and put-up numbers on our scoreboard, not just run around on the field.

Chapter 9: Stewardship — Faithfully Managing Time, Talent, and Treasure

There is a difference between busy and productive. The bee and the mosquito are both busy. But the bee is praised, and the mosquito swatted. There is no reward for busy—just, "Well done good and faithful servant."

#1 Start with the end in mind

> Oh, that they were wise, *that* they understood this, *That* they would consider their latter end! — *Deuteronomy 32:29 (NKJV)*

Alfred Nobel was the inventor of dynamite, an invention that made him a vast fortune. Later in Alfred's life his brother passed away. When reading his brother's obituary, he found that the reporter had made a mistake and thought Alfred had passed away. What he read horrified him. The obituary railed on Alfred as a man that invented death through his explosives and that he amassed a great fortune by creating weapons that killed. What he read bothered him so much that he set out to change what people would remember him by. He dedicated a large portion of his wealth to creating an award that would be given to people to recognize good that they did to better mankind. The award was named after him. The Nobel peace prize.

Alfred had the rare opportunity to see what the end of his life would be. He saw his tombstone epitaph before he died so to speak. As a result, he made deliberate changes. He defined his end zone of how he wanted to be remembered. To define your end zone, you have to ask yourself, "What really matters when all is said and done? What do I want to be remembered for?"

#2 Write It

We looked at the importance of a goal but that is not enough. The goal is clearly marked on the field. A base is at home plate. The large goal on the soccer field. We need to move from an idea to a written goal.

> Then the Lord answered me and said: "Write the vision And make *it* plain on tablets, That he may run who reads it." — *Habakkuk 2:2 (NKJV)*

Writing goals, defining an end zone, isn't something a motivational speaker came up with for a self-help book. It was God's idea. The reason it works in the corporate world is because it was God's idea. Only 5% of people have goals and only 3% have them in writing. Just get a goal and jump to the top 5%. Write it down and look out. J.C. Penny said, "Give me a stock clerk with a goal and I will give you a man that will make history. Give me a man without a goal and I will give you a stock clerk."

Time Magazine once did an article on a man named John Goddard: When he was 15, he heard his grandmother say, "I wish I would have done that when I was younger." Then and there he decided that when he approached the end of his life he would never have to say, "I wish I would have." He pulled out a sheet of paper and wrote down 127 goals, end zones that he wanted to achieve in his life:

- 17 mountains to climb
- 10 rivers to explore
- Become an eagle scout
- Pilot license
- Ride horse in Rose bowl parade
- Drive in a submarine
- Retrace travels of Marco polo
- Read Bible cover to cover
- Read entire encyclopedia of Britannica
- Read entire works of Shakespeare, Charles Dickens, Plato, and others
- Get married
- Have children – he had 5
- Purse a career in medicine
- Serve as missionary for his church

John Goddard accomplished 120 of the 127 goals before his death and over 500 goals he had set as he updated his list throughout his lifetime! The power of goals in writing!

Jesus knew his mission. He had a clearly defined written goal for his life. At the beginning of His ministry, he visited the synagogue in his hometown and open the scroll of Isaiah and read this verse. It was the public declaration of His mission statement from the Father.

> "The Spirit of the Lord *is* upon Me, Because He has anointed Me To preach the gospel to *the* poor; He has sent Me to heal the brokenhearted, To proclaim liberty to *the* captives, And recovery of sight to *the* blind, To set at liberty those who are oppressed; To proclaim the acceptable year of the Lord."
> — *Luke 4:18-19 (NKJV)*

He knew his end zone. When it was all said and done, he could say, "It is finished." *(John 17:4, 19:30 NKJV)* Most people can never say "it is finished" because they never knew what it was they were supposed to start. Take time to seek God, search your heart, and refine partnership with God as you define meaningful goals.

When defining your goals do three things:

- **Put them in writing**

- **Give yourself a deadline** – In Hebrew Methuselah's Name means, "when he is dead it shall come." Noah had a grandfather, and it was Methuselah. Noah knew that when grandpa kicked the bucket, he had better have the Ark built and ready to go because it "whatever that was" was coming when grandpa died. It's not a coincidence that the exact year he died is the year the flood came.

- **Keep them where you can see them** – we keep valuable what we keep visible

- **Review them often**

On the Element Staff we use OKRs – which are Objective by Key Results – It is a clear way of not just setting goals but measuring their results by the outcomes. We review these monthly as a team which keeps it visible and therefore it remains valuable. If you are new to the Element staff, you will learn more about this as you on board. If you are looking to learn more about OKRs I recommend a book by John Doer (what a great last name), *Measure What Matters*.

#3 Plan It

> The plans of the diligent *lead* surely to plenty, But *those of* everyone *who is* hasty, surely to poverty. — *Proverbs 21:5 (NKJV)*

Everyone who is successful in an area of life had a plan to get there. The people who fail are the ones who never had a plan. In fact, you might have heard the cliché, "Failing to plan is planning to fail." For example, I have met many people who struggle with finances. I ask them, "Can I see your financial plan or budget?" Never once in 35-years of ministry has anyone failing at finances ever produced a financial plan or written budget to show me. If you don't plan where your money goes someone else will. Same with time. "Where did the time go?" Failing to plan is planning to fail.

The most often used excuse I hear from people who don't have a plan is they don't have time to make a plan. But they are actually lying to themselves and believing their own lie. Recent data shows the average American watch's 294 minutes of TV a day and spends another four to five hours a day on their phones (between TV and the phone they are working another fulltime job). Everyone has time it's just that most people choose to squander it in things that don't matter much. Logically speaking saying you don't have time makes as much sense as saying, "I don't have time to stop and put gas into my car." You are going to stop eventually. Why not choose when. The stop will be much shorter and cost much less if you intentionally stop from time to time for gas. I once read that one minute of planning will save two minutes of execution.

Here are some tips on planning your time:

3. Time Blocks

My schedule is pretty much the same every working week. I break each day into time blocks. We get more done in focused chunks of time rather than in little, short bursts here and there.

- Plan A time for A projects – when you are most productive and creative

- Plan B time for B projects – good but less demanding tasks

Mornings for me are my A time (most productive). I am at my best creatively, so that is when I start my day with God and write messages, podcasts, books, and do thinking time. I rarely do any meetings before 11am because I reserve this time for what requires my greatest focus.

So, my week every morning—Tues, Wed, Thurs, Fri, Sat—from 8:00–10:30 is writing. Rarely is there an exception (if there is, it's either a week I am not preaching that weekend, or I am ahead on message writing, or it's an emergency I need to be a part of dealing with).

Tuesdays from 11:30–3:00 is always Executive Team.

Every Wed, Thurs, and Friday I fill my lunch with a meeting. Great book: *Never Eat Alone*. Most of the time it is with staff and core church leaders.

- Wed after lunch is creative meetings. We are working on message planning, creative elements for service, and big events like Christmas and Easter. I really enjoy this part of my job.

- Thursday once a month I have one-on-one time with each of my Executive Team members. This gives me personal time to be their pastor and provide direction and insight as their boss. I am able to coach and invest into the team that really is running the day-to-day of the church.

Chapter 9: Stewardship — Faithfully Managing Time, Talent, and Treasure

- On weeks I am not meeting 1:1, it's other meetings—usually meeting with a department team, brainstorming with a team for ministry growth, etc.

- Friday afternoon is rest and preparation for the weekend services.

- Saturday mornings is my final tweaks to the message and lots of extra prayer.

- Monday is my Sabbath rest. I protect this. Only personal things with family, friends, and personal to-dos. Rarely am I working on church on my Sabbath day.

After the week, hit the "Repeat." Sometimes it feels like ground hog day, but every week pastors have the rare job that after we finish our last Sunday service, we breathe a sigh of relief only to remember next weekend is coming.

All staff at Element are required to create time blocks with their schedules and review those with their direct report. When we have an underperforming staff member one of the first things we ask to see is their time blocks. Most of the time we find the problem right there. It's in their failure to plan that they are failing. Usually after we help them get their time blocks on track, we see an immediate uptick in their performance.

My Executive Team is very busy. More to do than enough time to do it all. In their 1:1 reports with me; they show me the last four weeks of time blocks and the next four weeks. This allows me to help them prioritize their time. Sometimes they need permission to say "no" to some things, so they have more time for others. Fresh eyes help us see with what we don't see. There is a saying in the writing community, "An author can't edit their own book." We don't have objectivity and clarity when we wrote it.

5. Time Audits

From time to time, we use track/log our time so we can see where it went. Imagine trying to manage your finances without a checkbook register or Quickbooks? You can't manage what you can't measure.

6. Practical Time Management Tips

> "I am the true vine, and My Father is the vinedresser. Every branch in Me that does not bear fruit He takes away; and every *branch* that bears fruit He prunes, that it may bear more fruit." — *John 15:1-2 (NKJV)*

Chapter 9: Stewardship — Faithfully Managing Time, Talent, and Treasure

To better manage our time, we need to look for the things that aren't fruitful and eliminate them or at least mitigate them.

#1 An Agenda for Every Meeting

One of the greatest amounts of time wasted is spent in ineffective meetings. To help meetings be more effective create in advance an agenda and the topics for review and the assigned amount of time to each. A great book on this topic is Patrick Lencioni's *Death by Meeting*.

For my Tuesday Executive Meetings one of our Executive Admins sends out email before the end of each week and asks all the Executives for their talking points and how much time they need. My Senior Executive Pastor then arranges the list, and they send out the agenda in advance. This keeps us on target and on time. We almost always get our whole list done.

When a large item pops up in the meeting, we place it a parking lot list and schedule more time for that topic.

#2 Checklists, Checklists, Checklists

When I get on airplanes, I see the cockpit door open and pilots going over the checklist. They have thousands of hours of flight time logged but still use the checklist. I don't want a pilot who says, "We don't need no stinking checklists. I have done this enough." That's when mistakes are made.

More time is wasted because of not following a simple checklist. Create a checklist for everything you do so that someone else could step in and do what you do if they followed a checklist.

#3 Schedule

I start my day by reviewing my schedule (My assistant texts me at the end of each day my schedule for the next day. I use it as a canned quick reference throughout the day). I set alarms for important meetings I don't want to forget. I am never late or miss appointments because of this. I have never missed one of my online Chinese lessons as of right now (which is more than 500 of them) because I set alarms on my phone.

Chapter 9: Stewardship — Faithfully Managing Time, Talent, and Treasure

#4 Emails

I check my emails for anything urgent or needs just a quick reply. I allow 15-minutes for this. This keeps staff empowered with the answers they need to do their jobs. THEN CLOSE (by this I mean turn off) MY EMAIL. Now if I don't, I would get distracted by all the dings that come in. If you stop and answer every email you lose momentum. I suggest three time blocks a day for emails. First thing in morning, before or after lunch, and at the end of the day before you go. For this allow an amount of time such as 30-60 minutes.

We have a "48-hour" rule on staff at Element (unfortunately not all staff are proficient at this, but we are getting better) meaning that all emails must be given a reply in that time. Even if it's just to say, "I got it. Can I get back to you by this Friday?" It is okay to ask for more time, but we must get back. EVERYONE matters to GOD, therefore every email (because there is a person behind it) matters to us.

Stewardship is not a one-time task but a lifelong journey of faithfulness and intentionality. As you reflect on the time, talents, and treasures God has entrusted to you, remember that He calls you to be faithful with what you have now before receiving more. Your stewardship shapes not only your own life but the lives of those around you and the future of the Church. Embrace your role as a steward of time with joy and diligence, knowing that your faithfulness honors God and advances His kingdom. May you steward well, run your race with purpose, and one day hear the words, "Well done, good and faithful servant."

Talent

1. Talent: Growth Requires Preparation

> "For the *kingdom of heaven is* like a man traveling to a far country, *who* called his own servants and delivered his goods to them. And to one he gave five talents, to another two, and to another one, to each according to his own ability; and immediately he went on a journey." — *Matthew 25:14–15 (NKJV)*

When you grow, you reach limits. Baby clothes were cute but eventually you outgrew them. Each stage of life presents new boundaries. You can either continue growing and upgrade or stop growing altogether. I once read that a baby shark will only grow as large as its aquarium allows.

Chapter 9: Stewardship — Faithfully Managing Time, Talent, and Treasure

Proper Planning Prevents Poor Performance

> The plans of the diligent *lead* surely to plenty, but *those of* everyone *who is* hasty, surely to poverty. — *Proverbs 21:5 (NKJV)*

David declared, "[I have] killed the lion and the bear... *(1 Sam. 17:36 NKJV)."* He was faithful in the place where he was before he faced Goliath. Be faithful in the unseen moments. Leaders are readers; they learn and prepare. When I was about 24 and youth pastoring, I created a folder entitled, *"When I Pastor."* As I learned from the good, the bad, and the ugly of ministry I would make notes and put those into that folder for reminders and a future reference. All my learning experiences were not being wasted. They were being captured to prepare me for what God was preparing me for. It became a practical foundation for curating insights and resources that have shaped me into much of what I am as a pastor today.

God Prepares Us for What He Is Preparing for Us

Growth is intentional. Tools like an Individual Development Plan (IDP) help us grow with intentionality. Like one leader said, "There is a difference between growing old and growing up. Growing old is automatic but growing up is a choice.

Everyone grows old but not everyone grows up." All our leadership staff with their leadership oversight, work to build a custom IDP. This is a good tool to help intentionality in growth. These IDPs are reviewed regularly to discuss progress and make adjustments in the plan as necessary. IDPs are more fluid than static. Any world class athlete has a growth plan from their coach. They don't show up to practice and wonder what they are going to work on that day and certainly no world class team shows up to a game without a playbook. Our IDPs are part of our game plan and play book to help us win and to be added to the giants of faith recorded in Hebrews Chapter 11.

Ted Williams once said, *"Ballplayers are not born great. They're not born great hitters or pitchers or managers, and luck isn't a big factor. No one has come up with a substitute for hard work.... Baseball gives every American boy a chance to excel."* Excellence is cultivated over time, not given spontaneously.

Jesus was thirty years old before He entered ministry. He spent thirty years preparing for three and a half years of ministry—approximately ten years of preparation for each year of ministry. Jacob's son Joseph trained for thirteen years between Potiphar's house and prison—for leadership in Pharaoh's palace. Moses spent forty years in the back side of the desert. Joshua spent forty years under Moses' leadership wandering around in the desert. If you let Him, you will find that God never wastes desert seasons in our life.

The Chinese bamboo tree offers a powerful lesson. For the first four years, it remains only a tiny shoot above the ground. But in the fifth year, it can grow up to eighty feet tall. The growth was happening all along—beneath the surface, building a massive root system—before it finally shoots up.

2.Talent: God's Plan for Leadership

#1 God Prepares Us for What He Has Prepared for Us

> His parents went to Jerusalem every year at the Feast of the Passover. And when He was twelve years old, they went up to Jerusalem according to the custom of the feast. — *Luke 2:41-42 (NKJV)*

This is the only insight we have into Jesus' life before He began full-time ministry at thirty. Jesus was twelve years old. What we see here is God the Father preparing His Son for leadership, and it represents eighteen years of preparation to lead for three years. The longer the preparation, the bigger the assignment God is trusting us with.

During my time at Bible school, I was placed over the maintenance at Church On The Move, in Tulsa Oklahoma. I loved it but after Bible school, while many of my friends were promoted to what seemed like more exciting roles in other churches, I was still the janitor. I called my ministry, "Totally Triumphant Toilets." Sounded more important than janitor. At first, it was difficult to understand. But looking back, I see that God was using that season of private work to prepare me for greater public service. I wouldn't trade those days for anything. God did deep things in my soul that still are foundations in my life today. I am a better leader because of it.

Ever wonder why the Bible mentions that Jesus was "twelve years old?" All numbers inside of scripture have meaning. For example, three is number of perfections thus the trinity is three, six is the number of man because man was created on the sixth day. The antichrist is 666 because it's the number of man three times, which the antichrist will be perfectly imperfect. Twelve is the number of divine governments. We see the twelve tribes of Israel, twelve disciples representing the New Testament, and twenty-four elders around the throne which represent all of God's people from Genesis to Revelation. *(Rev. 4:4)* The number of twelve is divine government and leadership. This footnote of Jesus being twelve is significant.

Chapter 9: Stewardship — Faithfully Managing Time, Talent, and Treasure

> For unto us a Child is born, Unto us a Son is given; And the government will be upon His shoulder. And His name will be called Wonderful...Of the increase of *His government...There will be* no end... — Isaiah 9:6-7 (NKJV)

The government and leadership are the weights we carry. *Genesis 22:6 NKJV* shows Abraham placing the wood upon his son Isaac's shoulders as they ascended Mount Moriah. God the Father would allow the wood of the cross upon the shoulders of His son Jesus as he ascended that very same mountain. Leadership is the weight we carry upon our shoulders for the people and often because of people. The Old Testament priests had a plate on each shoulder with the names of each of the twelve tribes inscribed upon it. *(Exodus 28:12 NKJV)* Why? Leaders bare the burned of people. Upon the chest of the priest, they wore a breastplate with twelve gemstones that represented the twelve tribes of Israel. *(Exodus 28:29 NKJV)* Why? The people must be on our heart so we can bare their burdens. If we bare burdens and people are not on our heart we will be crushed under the weight of ministry.

Always remember this Jesus carried a cross before He wore a crown. As a leader there is always a cross before a crown.

#2 A Leader's Lid Is the Tolerance of Pain

In the book *Leadership Pain* by Dr. Sam Chan, this principle is explored in depth. A must read for every leader.

> But Jesus answered and said, "You do not know what you ask. Are you able to drink the cup that I am about to drink, and be baptized with the baptism that I am baptized with?" They said to Him, "We are able." — *Matthew 20:22 (NKJV)*

Leaders carry crosses before they carry crowns. The cup of suffering is real. Paul speaks of knowing Christ through the fellowship of His sufferings (Phil 3:10). The number one lid of leadership isn't talent but tolerance for pain. Leaders suffer for the people, with the people, and by the people. Leadership includes a baptism of death. The Air Force's special forces called PJ's Para-rangers have a creed I feel expresses the same principle: *"So others may live."* Every death in Christ has a resurrection.

> So He said to them, "You will indeed drink My cup, and be baptized with the baptism that I am baptized with; but to sit on My right hand and on My left is not Mine to give, but *it is for those* for whom it is PREPARED by My Father." — *Matthew 20:23 (NKJV)*

Chapter 9: Stewardship — Faithfully Managing Time, Talent, and Treasure

Endurance in pain and preparation shapes the character and readiness of a leader for the assignments God has prepared for them. I wonder how many assignments God intended to give me that He wasn't able to because I was under prepared?

#3 Leaders Feed Before They Lead

> When they had finished the days, as they returned, the Boy Jesus lingered behind in Jerusalem. And Joseph and His mother did not know *it*; but supposing Him to have been in the company, they went a day's journey and sought Him among *their* relatives and acquaintances. — *Luke 2:43-44 (NKJV)*

Joseph and Mary went to the Passover to worship as required but did not perceive the Passover Lamb with them. They left Him behind, and it wasn't until a day later that they realized He was missing. Leaders must be careful not to come to church or ministry and leave Jesus behind. Take Him with you into every space, every interaction. The danger in ministry is becoming so focused on the work of the Lord that we forget the Lord of the work. How frightening it is to travel thinking you have Jesus with you, but in reality, you left Him behind. I have done this too many times and probably will again. Thank the Lord His mercies are new every morning.

What does your personal devotional life look like? What books are you reading? Leaders must feed themselves spiritually before they can truly lead others.

We use a term at Element with our staff called, "Front Row Leadership." Whether or not you are sitting physically on the front row of the church service you are in front of someone who is watching you. Therefore, lean in, take notes, Amen the message. Set the tone that leaders are leaners because leadership is contagious and is caught more than taught. But if you are scrolling on your phone and looking bored that will also be contagious. Remember the game you may have played as kids "monkey see monkey do?" Well, leadership is the same, people do what they see us do, not so much what they hear us say. The goal of great leadership is that our words and our actions are in alignment and there is no gap between the two.

> So when they did not find Him, they returned to Jerusalem, seeking Him. Now so it was *that* after three days they found Him in the temple, sitting in the midst of the teachers, both listening to them and asking them questions. — *Luke 2:45-46 (NKJV)*

When you realize He is missing, return to the place where you last encountered Him. *Revelation 2:5* reminds the church at Ephesus: *Remember, Return, and Repeat.* Leaders must be intentional about returning to the presence of the Lord and leaning in when they have lost connection.

#4 Leaders Are Lifelong Learners

Jesus was listening and asking questions. A Chinese proverb says it well, *"A man reveals his knowledge by his answer, but his wisdom by his questions."* True leadership is drawn out by curiosity and the willingness to learn. I cannot pastor my staff beyond the invitation they give me through their questions.

I like how one pastor I know says it to his leadership staff, *"If you never ask me questions you are either proud or perfect, and I know you aren't perfect, so you must be proud."* Church planters or leaders who seek resources but not wisdom often receive neither. Those who pursue the leader's time, those who seek wisdom through questions, are the ones who grow and gain insight and also are the ones who get both wisdom and resources.

#5 Leaders Prioritize Around Their Purpose

> So when they saw Him, they were amazed; and His mother said to Him, "Son, why have You done this to us? Look, Your father and I have sought You anxiously." And He said to them, "Why did you seek Me? Did you not know that I must be about My Father's business?" — *Luke 2:48-49 (NKJV)*

Joseph and Mary were stressed because they were distracted from their purpose. Most stress is the by-product of doing the wrong things and neglecting the right things. Leaders must learn to prioritize around their calling and purpose.

> "Everyone is looking for you...Let us go into the next towns..." — *Mark 1:37-38 (NKJV)*

Luke records three must-dos of Jesus: first, His Father's business *(Luke 2:49 NKJV)* "I must be about my Father's business"; second, preaching the Gospel *(Luke 4:43 NKJV)* "I must preach to the other cities..."; and third, offering Himself on the cross *(Luke 9:22 NKJV)* "I must suffer many things...".

> But they did not understand the statement which He spoke to them. Then He went down with them and came to Nazareth, and was

subject to them...And Jesus increased in wisdom and stature, and in favor with God and men. — *Luke 2:50-52 (NKJV)*

#6 God Uses Imperfect Leaders to Perfect Us

Joseph and Mary did not yet understand the significance of what Jesus had said or done. Yet, Jesus submitted to their authority and went back with them. Leaders must sometimes submit to guidance even when they understand more about a subject than their leaders. The result of this submission was seen in verse *Luke 2:52 NIV*, "Jesus grew in wisdom and stature, and in favor with God and man."

He was subject even when he knew more about the subject than those leading him. A wise leader recognizes their weaknesses and staffs accordingly. Do not compare your strengths against your leader's weaknesses. God uses imperfect leadership to cultivate growth and maturity in those under it.

3. Talent: The Power of Relationship

Mathematicians tell us that if you take two pieces of Legos, each with eight snaps, and connect them together, you get 24 different possibilities. Add just one more, and suddenly you have 1,060 possibilities to connect these three Legos. Add three more, for a total of six, and you have over 102,981,500 possibilities.

We are like these Legos. Each of us has the ability to "snap" together relationally with others. When we do, we create endless possibilities. Our possibilities expand in direct proportion to the people we are connected with.

> After these things the Lord appointed seventy others also, and sent them two by two before His face into every city and place where He Himself was about to go... — *Luke 10:1 (NKJV)*

Jesus connected and "snapped" relationships together to go ahead to the places He was about to go. Together, they accomplished great things, and then Christ Himself showed up to do even greater.

#1 Relationships Are God's Resources That Produce His Results

In my life, every new possibility can be traced to a relationship. There are no accidental relationships. We rise or fall to the level of friendships we choose. I intentionally find people who have what I want and pursue those relationships. Some people are like firefighters, others like pyros—lighting the fires of vision and passion in your life. Others will try to put out the fires.

> And the Lord God said, "*It is* not good that man should be alone; I will make him a helper comparable to him..." — *Genesis 2:18 (NKJV)*

As we look back to the section, *The First "Not Good"* in Chapter 5 of this book, we are reminded in Hebrew, "not good" is *lo tob*, meaning it's inherently bad for Adam to be alone. The first time God said something was not good was not when people sinned—it was when He saw Adam alone. This teaches a profound truth: relationships are essential to fulfilling God's design.

#2 God Made Us with Certain Needs He Chose Not to Meet

God made Adam with a need for someone else because He had given him a mission:

> "Be fruitful and multiply (1x0=0); fill the earth and subdue it; have dominion..." — *Genesis 1:28 (NKJV)*

We are designed to pursue relationships to accomplish God's purpose. I intentionally reach out to high-capacity leaders and introduce myself, *"Hi, I am Erik Lawson. I want to learn from you."* Most people don't know this about me—it's not a boast, but a strategy that has helped me learn from some of today's most impactful leaders.

For example, I have had the opportunity to spend time with leaders such as General Norman Schwarzkopf, the late President Gerald Ford, Bill Gates, Gen. Colin Powell, late President Ronald Reagan, Michael Dell, founder of Dell computers, the late Steve Jobs, NBA's greatest Michael Jordan, former CEO of GE Jack Welch, Elon Musk, and the list goes on. I have had opportunity to sit with each of them and learn. Now for the record none of them responded to my emails, phone calls, and a few have restraining orders against me (just joking) so I had to do the next best thing and that is read their books, watch their interviews, read their articles. I still spent time with them to glean their wisdom—it just wasn't in person. Leaders are readers! If you are not reading you are not leading, at least not leading well.

#3 Even Giant Killers Get Tired

> When the Philistines were at war again with Israel, David and his servants with him went down and fought against the Philistines; and David grew faint. Then Ishbi-Benob, who

> *was* one of the sons of the giant, the weight of whose bronze spear *was* three hundred *shekels*, who was bearing a new *sword*, thought he could kill David. But Abishai...came to his aid, and struck the Philistine and killed him. — *2 Samuel 21:15-17 (NKJV)*

David grew tired. Every Christian gets weary and will eventually face a giant too big to defeat alone. Goliath's brother, Ishbi-Benob, sought revenge and thought he could kill David.

The giant you have killed in the past may have a brother waiting in your future. No matter how many giants you have defeated, there will always be one too big to fight alone.

What would have happened if David had decided he didn't need his group and went into battle alone? He would have died. His lamp would have been snuffed out. But because he battled with a group of mighty men, Abishai was there to defend him. Who are the mighty men and women in your life when you are weary and cannot lift your sword against the giant?

#4 Even Giant Killers Have Blind Spots

> Then the men of David swore to him, saying, "You shall go out no more with us to battle, lest you quench the lamp of Israel..." — 2 Samuel 21:17 (NKJV)

David had grown old and rusty in battle. Billy-Bob's spear was only half the weight of Goliath's, and yet it proved dangerous. Strength alone is not enough. Knowing your strength may be your greatest weakness, and knowing your weakness may be your greatest strength.

Who in your life loves you enough to tell you the truth?

> Faithful *are* the wounds of a friend, But the kisses of an enemy *are* deceitful... — Proverbs 27:6 (NKJV)

I once preached a sermon with my zipper down (for the record it was not at Element Church but a leadership conference—okay, even more embarrassing). A faithful friend pointed it out, but unfortunately not until after the sermon was done. I guess better late than never. I am reminded that honest feedback is a gift, even if it's uncomfortable.

Chapter 9: Stewardship — Faithfully Managing Time, Talent, and Treasure

4. Talent: Finish Strong

When I started out in ministry I heard a startling statistic. At first, I didn't believe it and it is this: only one in ten who start in ministry will finish in ministry. That is a 90% dropout rate. Ministry has the highest mortality rate of any profession. Sadly after 35 plus years of seeing friends, fellow minsters, and ministry staff drop out of the race I have come to believe this number is true.

> Now in a great house there are not only articles of gold and silver, but also others of wood and of earthenware; and some are for especially honorable, and others for common use. If therefore a man keeps himself clear of these latter, he himself will be for especially honorable use, consecrated, fit for the Master's service, and fully equipped for every good work..." — 2 Timothy 2:20-21 (Weymouth New Testament WNT)

The Bible makes clear there are Christians who live their lives in an uncommon way. These are vessels of honor, consecrated for special purposes. Others live as vessels of common usefulness. I want to be a vessel of honor—a Hall of Famer. I'm sure you do too.

What about failure? Unfortunately, the body of Christ sometimes discards those who fail. But God doesn't. Just ask David or Samson. Peter had a significant moral failure when he denied Jesus. Yet fifty days later after Jesus restored him, he preached a powerful sermon on the Day of Pentecost, and 3,000 were saved. David continued as king, and Jesus came from his lineage.

Many point to *1 Corinthians 9:24, 27* as an example that a leaders failure "disqualifies" them from ministry. This is not the context because at the beginning Paul's says, "the prize."

> Do you not know that those who run in a race all run, but one receives the prize? Run in such a way that you may obtain *it*...But I discipline my body and bring *it* into subjection, lest, when I have preached to others, I myself should become disqualified. — *1 Corinthians 9:24,27 (NKJV)*

Restoration and healing are essential.

> Brethren, if a man is overtaken in any trespass, you who *are* spiritual restore such a one in a spirit of gentleness, considering yourself lest you also be tempted. — *Galatians 6:1 (NKJV)*

Chapter 9: Stewardship — Faithfully Managing Time, Talent, and Treasure

David recognized that even his sin produced new qualifications for God's work in his life.

> Create in me a clean heart, O God, And renew a steadfast spirit within me. Do not cast me away from Your presence, And do not take Your Holy Spirit from me. Restore to me the joy of Your salvation, And uphold me *by Your* generous Spirit. *Then* I will teach transgressors Your ways, And sinners shall be converted to You. — *Psalms 51:10-13 (NKJV)*

Sin carries consequences for sure.

> But if you do not do so, then take note, you have sinned against the LORD; and be sure your sin will find you out. — *Numbers 32:23 (NKJV)*

It's not God tracking us down but sin itself that hunts and haunts us. Leadership is built on the pace of trust, and a failure in leadership can create unintended ramifications that bring a lifetime of pain (just ask David about his parenting struggles, Absalom's rebellion, and the betrayal of his once-trusted adviser Ahithophel, and the list goes on). Even so, in the hands of God, He can restore and redeem a fallen leader. This is the heart of the gospel, and it should also be the heart of the church.

Treasure

We are now on the last of the three things we are called to steward: time, talent, and treasure.

I want to share some very practical thoughts regarding personal finances, because if you cannot manage your own money well, chances are you will not manage church money well either. Poor financial stewardship at home is often a major cause of pain and distraction at work. In fact, it is one of the reasons some people leave ministry early. Some quit ministries altogether in pursuit of higher-paying jobs. But more money is not always the answer. It starts with getting better at managing what you already have.

If you are bad with your money now, no matter how much more you make, you will still be bad with it. Those are not my words—those are the words of Jesus. I have seen this same struggle with volunteers. Many stop serving because they feel the need to work more hours to earn more money. But the truth is, they often just need to become better stewards of what they already possess. If Satan can get you out of God's will because you feel you need more money, then he will always look for ways to keep you in financial pressure.

Chapter 9: Stewardship — Faithfully Managing Time, Talent, and Treasure

> He who *is* faithful in *what is* least is faithful also in much; and he who is unjust in *what is* least is unjust also in much. Therefore if you have not been faithful in the unrighteous mammon, who will commit to your trust the true *riches?* — *Luke 16:10-12 (NKJV)*

Jesus understood our need for money and the way it impacts every part of our lives. Out of the 38 parables He taught, 16 dealt with money and possessions. The Bible contains about 500 verses on prayer, fewer than 500 verses on faith, but more than 2,000 verses on money and possessions—four times as many.

We are going to look at five principles that will help us become better stewards and step into a new level of financial freedom.

> He also said to His disciples: "There was a certain rich man who had a steward, and an accusation was brought to him that this man was wasting his goods. So he called him and said to him, 'What is this I hear about you? Give an account of your stewardship, for you can no longer be steward.' Then the steward said within himself, 'What shall I do?' ... He who *is* faithful in *what is* least is faithful also in much; and he who is unjust in *what is* least is unjust also in much.... Therefore if

you have not been faithful in the unrighteous mammon, who will commit to your trust the true *riches?* ... No servant can serve two masters; for either he will hate the one and love the other, or else he will be loyal to the one and despise the other. You cannot serve God and mammon." — *Luke 16:1-3, 10-13 (NKJV)*

Three Things We Learn About Money

1. God Has More Than Enough

"There was a certain rich man who had a steward..." — *Luke 16:1 (NKJV)*

Our God is El Shaddai—the God of more than enough. I like how one pastor says it, "God is El Shaddai not El Cheapo!"

Our heavenly Father is not like little Johnny's dad. Little Johnny was once in math class when the teacher asked him to solve an addition problem: "Johnny, if you had $5 and you asked your father for $3 more, how many dollars would you have?" Johnny replied, "I would have $5." The teacher said, "You don't know your arithmetic." Johnny answered, "You don't know my dad."

That's not our Heavenly Father. He is generous. He is a gracious provider. Our God is always more than enough.

2. Mammon Makes False Promises

When we worry about money, it is a symptom of misplaced trust. We worry because we mistakenly believe that our job or our bank account is our source. Mammon—the ancient Syrian god of riches—always tries to make promises that only God Himself can fulfill.

#1 Mammon Promises Security

> Keep your lives free from the love of money and be content with what you have, because God has said, "Never will I leave you; never will I forsake you." So we say with confidence, "The Lord is my helper; I will not be afraid." — *Hebrews 13:5-6 (NIV)*

Contentment is not the fulfillment of what you want, but the realization of what you already have.

A rabbi in a small Jerusalem apartment had only a chair, a desk, and a bed. A wealthy woman visiting from New York asked, "Rabbi, is this your house?" "Yes," he replied. "Well, where is your furniture?"

The rabbi smiled and said, "Where is your furniture?" She replied, "I didn't bring my furniture; I am just traveling. "Ah," he said with a smile, "So am I."

#2 Mammon Promises Identity

We buy things we cannot afford to impress people who don't care because we think our possessions define who we are.

> Then he said, "Beware! Guard against every kind of greed. Life is not measured by how much you own.'" — *Luke 12:15 (New Living Translation NLT)*

We keep "stats" on ourselves, comparing, accumulating, and hoping our identity comes from wealth. The word status is keeping "Stats" on "Us." Thus, status.

#3 Mammon Promises Happiness

> Those who love money will never have enough. How meaningless to think that wealth brings true happiness! — *Ecclesiastes 5:10 (NLT)*

> Command those who are rich in this present world not to be arrogant nor to put their

hope in wealth, which is so uncertain, but to put their hope in God..." — *1 Timothy 6:17 (NIV)*

Paul speaks directly to those who place their hope in money. The problem is that rich is a moving target. Surveys show people earning $30k a year feel rich if they could just make $74k a year; people earning $50k feel need to make $100k to feel rich; high-income earners making a million a year need to make $5 million a year. See the pattern here? If we don't feel rich, we keep chasing it and are never satisfied.

The truth is: we are already rich.

- 700 million people (10%) live on less than $2 a day—$730 per year.

- 1.9 billion people (46%) live on less than $5.50 a day—$2,000 per year.

- The average daily cost of Starbucks in the U.S. is higher than what much of the world earns in a year.

Globally, the average home is 743 square feet. One billion people don't own a single pair of shoes. Yet, in wealthier societies, people still pursue possessions, thinking they will bring happiness. But happiness is not a purchase; it is a person. It is found in God, not in the accumulation of things.

3. We Are Managers Not Owners

> He also said to His disciples: "There was a certain rich man who had a steward..."' — Luke 16:1 (NKJV)

A steward is simply *"a person employed to manage another's property."*

We run into all kinds of problems when we start thinking it's our time, our talent, our treasure—even our very lives. Everything we have is from God and for God *(Rev. 4:11 NKJV)*. This should radically change the way we think about life.

As a staff member or volunteer at Element, we are not owners of God's church—we are stewards. We manage what belongs to Him.

God Is Looking for Increase.

> Where there is no vision, the people perish...
> — *Proverbs 29:18 (KJV)*

Chapter 9: Stewardship — Faithfully Managing Time, Talent, and Treasure

Stewardship begins with vision. Without it, we drift. Too often we navigate life like Alice in Wonderland when she is lost and asks the Cheshire cat for directions:

> **Alice:** "Would you tell me, please, which way I ought to go from here?"
>
> **The Cat:** "That depends a good deal on where you want to get to."
>
> **Alice:** "I don't much care where."
>
> **The Cat:** "Then it doesn't much matter which way you go."
>
> **Alice:** "...so long as I get somewhere."
>
> **The Cat:** "Oh, you're sure to do that, if only you walk long enough."

Many of us live this way financially, too—just walking long enough, hoping to "get somewhere." But biblical stewardship requires intentional vision.

4. Start By Redefining Wealth

Most people define wealth by how much money they make: "If I earn $50,000 a year, I'll be wealthy." "Maybe $100,000 a year will make me wealthy..."

But that's navigating with the wrong definition.

#1 Wealth Is Not How Much Money You Make

Wealth is how much money makes *you.* In other words, how much of your money is working for you—saved, invested, producing more money. If you haven't read Robert Kiyosakis book *Rich Dad, Poor Dad* I highly recommend it. In fact, when my kids were teenagers and wanted money, I paid each of them to read this book. Fortunately, all three of them did and now as adults they are all doing well managing the money God entrusts to them.

Imagine having ten apples. You may feel wealthy with apples, but once you eat them, they're gone. True wealth is not in how many apples you have, but in how many apple trees you have. Trees keep producing fruit, and you never run out. Wise is the person who would plant the apples seeds they have now for a harvest in their future.

Chapter 9: Stewardship — Faithfully Managing Time, Talent, and Treasure

#2 Wealth Is How Long You Can Go Without Working for Money

Another way to measure wealth is to ask: *How long could I live on what I have if I stopped working today?* If the flow of income dried up, how long before the savings, investments, and fruit of wise stewardship can sustain you?

This mindset shifts us from ownership to stewardship. The goal isn't to cling to what we have but to grow what God has entrusted us with—for His purposes and His glory.

#3 Wealth Is Being Rich with Good Works

Having a lot of money doesn't make a person rich—they just have a lot of money. We are only truly rich when we understand and use money according to God's purposes for it.

> Command those who are rich in this present age not to be haughty, nor to trust in uncertain riches but in the living God, who gives us richly all things to enjoy. *Let them do good, that they be rich in good works, ready to give, willing to share, storing up for themselves a good foundation for the time to come, that they may lay hold on eternal life."* — *1 Timothy 6:17–19 (NKJV)*

God blesses us so that we might be a blessing to others and help build His kingdom. We are to be rich in good works. There are many who are cash rich but spiritually poor. True riches are found in using what God has entrusted to us to strengthen His Church. He also wants us to enjoy what He has given us—while remembering it is not meant for ourselves alone.

The Laodicean church was the last of the seven churches Jesus addressed in Revelation. They thought they were rich, but Jesus had a very different view.

> "Because you say, 'I am rich, have become wealthy, and have need of nothing'—and do not know that you are wretched, miserable, poor, blind, and naked." — *Revelation 3:17 (NKJV)*

The danger of material wealth is we can get lulled into thinking we have need of nothing. They were materially rich but spiritually bankrupt. Jesus says, that where our treasure is there our heart will be also. Tithing and generosity above the tithe is the antidote to this issue. When we give to the Lord our heart is in His house.

Chapter 9: Stewardship — Faithfully Managing Time, Talent, and Treasure

Let Talk About Investing

Building wealth is as simple as eating an apple. An apple meets your immediate physical need, but it also carries potential for the future. At its core are seeds—seeds that, when planted, can grow into apple trees, which in turn produce more apples.

Every dollar you hold is like that apple. It can meet your needs today, but it also contains seeds for your future. If you spend $50, you don't just lose $50—you lose the *potential* of what that $50 could have earned. Over 30 years at 12%, that same $50 has the power to grow into $1,800.

> "The Lord will command the blessing on you in your storehouses and in all to which you set your hand..." — *Deuteronomy 28:8 (NKJV)*

God can't bless what you haven't saved in your "barn." He blesses what you set aside, what you steward, and what you prepare.

> The Lord will open to you His good treasure, the heavens, to give the rain to your land in its season, and to bless all the work of your hand. You shall lend to many nations, but you shall not borrow. — *Deuteronomy 28:12 (NKJV)*

Even Jesus, in the parable of the talents, rebuked the servant who buried what he was given instead of at least lending it out to gain interest. Investing is simply putting your money to work. When I invest, I'm not just making money—I'm helping companies grow. I'm lending rather than borrowing.

Biblical Principles for Investing

#1 Don't try to get rich quick

> An inheritance gained hastily at the beginning Will not be blessed at the end. — *Proverbs 20:21 (NKJV)*

Avoid the pressure of "once-in-a-lifetime" opportunities. Real wealth doesn't come overnight. Do your homework, seek wise counsel, and use experienced investment advisors if needed.

#2 Do your homework

> Through wisdom a house is built, And by understanding it is established; By knowledge the rooms are filled With all precious and pleasant riches. — *Proverbs 24:3-4 (NKJV)*

Chapter 9: Stewardship — Faithfully Managing Time, Talent, and Treasure

Study, read, and learn. Statistics show that only 10% of Americans will ever read a book on personal finance, yet 97% own at least one TV. No wonder one in four adults say they don't believe they will ever be able to retire.

Some great resources:

- *Rich Dad, Poor Dad* by Robert Kiyosaki

- *Money: Master the Game* by Tony Robbins

- Financial Peace University (Dave Ramsey's course – which we offer here at Element)

#3 Invest consistently

> Dishonest money dwindles away, but whoever gathers money little by little makes it grow. — *Proverbs 13:11 (NIV)*

Wealth is not built on big breaks but on consistency. Take advantage of retirement plans like a 401(k) or 403(b)—especially if your employer matches contributions.

It doesn't take a fortune to build a fortune—it takes faithfulness. For example, if a 20-year-old saves just $1.50 a day ($45 a month) and earns 12% (the stock market's historical average since 1929), by the age of 65 they would have nearly $1,000,000.

I taught my children that every dollar is like a chicken. You can kill it and eat chicken nuggets—or you can keep it and let it lay eggs. Those eggs can be sold, and the process continues to multiply.

#4 Diversify

> Plant your seed in the morning and keep busy all afternoon, for you don't know if profit will come from one activity or another—or maybe both. — *Ecclesiastes 11:6 (NLT)*

Don't put all your eggs in one basket. Spread your investments across different assets, industries, and strategies. Index funds are a simple and proven way to diversify.

Let's Talk About Debt

We Shouldn't Waste It

> He also said to His disciples: "There was a certain rich man who had a steward, and an accusation was brought to him that this man was wasting his goods. So he called him and

> said to him, 'What is this I hear about you?'"
> — Luke 16:1–2 (NKJV)

One of the greatest wastes in life is debt. Not only do you lose money paying the bank interest, but you also lose the potential that money could have had to work for you.

> The rich rules over the poor, And the borrower *is* servant to the lender. — Proverbs 22:7 (NKJV)

Debt makes you a servant. It robs you of freedom, of opportunity, and even of peace.

Consider this story: George Phillips of Meridian, MS, was going to bed when his wife reminded him, he'd left the light on in the shed. When George opened the door, he discovered thieves in the act.

He called the police. "Is someone in your house?" they asked. George explained the situation. They told him all patrols were busy and advised him to lock the door until someone became available. Frustrated, he counted to 60 and called back.

"Hello," he said. "I just called about the people in my shed. Well, you don't have to worry about them anymore—I've just shot them all."

Within five minutes, three squad cars, an armed response unit, and an ambulance arrived. Of course, the thieves were caught red-handed. One officer asked, "I thought you said you'd shot them?" George calmly replied, "I thought you said there was nobody available."

Debt works the same way—it waits quietly until it owns you, stealing your resources and enslaving your freedom.

- The average American owes $8,100 in credit card debt.

- Paying the minimum of $324 per month at 19.8% interest takes 15 years to pay off, costing $5,500 in interest alone.

- If instead, you paid yourself $324 per month at a 12% return, in 15 years you'd have $162,000, and in 30 years, $1,132,000.

Debt doesn't just cost money—it costs your future. Don't let it rob you.

#1 Stop Spending Money You Don't Have

You can't get out of a hole if you keep shoveling. Stop digging. Do some "plastic surgery"—or as

Chapter 9: Stewardship — Faithfully Managing Time, Talent, and Treasure

Dave Ramsey calls it, a "plasectomy": cut up those credit cards.

Studies show we spend 23% more when using credit compared to cash.

> The wise have wealth and luxury, but fools spend whatever they get. — *Proverbs 21:20 (NLT)*

If a fool spends everything they get, then what do you call a person who spends money they don't even have? Ouch! Been there, done that.

Action Step: CUT UP YOUR CARDS. Use cash. Debit cards still work—and they won't bury you in debt.

#2 Build a Cash Reserve

A small emergency fund is your first defense. Start with $1,000—enough to cover most unexpected expenses so you won't reach for credit.

> Go to the ant, you sluggard! Consider her ways and be wise, Which, having no captain, Overseer or ruler, Provides her supplies in the summer, *And* gathers her food in the harvest. — *Proverbs 6:6–8 (NKJV)*

> The wise man saves for his future. — *Proverbs 21:20a (The Living Bible TLB)*

The wise save. The opposite? Fools spend. Don't spend everything you get.

Ask yourself: When extra money comes in, is your first thought *"What can I buy?"* or *"How can I save?"*

> And my God shall supply all your need according to His riches in glory by Christ Jesus. — *Philippians 4:19 (NKJV)*

We love to quote this verse when we're in financial trouble. But could it be that God already supplied the need before the crisis—through that extra income you spent? Joseph's miracle wasn't just surviving famine—it was hearing God beforehand and preparing during abundance.

#3 List Your Debts

The first step toward freedom is knowing what you owe. Write down every debt, the interest rate, the total owed, and the minimum payment.

Chapter 9: Stewardship — Faithfully Managing Time, Talent, and Treasure

Debt	Interest Rate	Total Owed	Minimum Payment
Sears	18%	$600	$24
Dillard's	18%	$1,200	$48
MasterCard	18%	$1,500	$60
Visa	18%	$1,800	$72
Discover	18%	$3,000	$120

When you can see it in black and white, it becomes real. Debt loses power when it's exposed to the light.

#4 Snowball Payments

Now we're going to pay this down much faster. Find an extra $50 a month—pack a lunch one day a week, skip a few coffees, or sell something you don't need.

If you're driving a car you can't afford, remember cars aren't status symbols—they're transportation. Sell the car, free up the money, and aim it at your debt.

Then apply the **Debt Snowball**:

1. Pay the minimum on all debts except the smallest one.

2. Add your extra money to that smallest balance until it's gone.

3. Roll that payment into the next debt.

4. Repeat until everything is paid off.

Here's how it works:

Debt	Total Owed	Minimum Payment	New Payment
Sears	$600	$24	$24 + $50 = $74
Dillard's	$1,200	$48	$48 + $74 = $122
MasterCard	$1,500	$60	$60 + $122 = $182

Chapter 9: Stewardship — Faithfully Managing Time, Talent, and Treasure

Visa	$1,800	$72	$72 + $182 = $254
Discover	$3,000	$120	$120 + $254 = $374

By following this plan, you'll be debt-free in just 2.8 years (32 months)—a savings of over 8 years compared to making minimum payments!

And here's the best part: once free, you can take that same $374 per month and start investing it. Instead of debt snowballing against you, your money begins to snowball for you.

Investing In Your ERA

> "There was a certain rich man who had a steward, and an accusation was brought to him that this man was wasting his goods. So he called him and said to him, 'What is this I hear about you? Give an account of your stewardship, for you can no longer be steward.' Then the steward said within himself, 'What shall I do? For my master is taking the stewardship away from me. I cannot dig; I am ashamed to beg.' ... He who *is* faithful in *what is* least is faithful also in

much; and he who is unjust in *what is* least is unjust also in much. Therefore if you have not been faithful in the unrighteous mammon, who will commit to your trust the true *riches?*... No servant can serve two masters; for either he will hate the one and love the other, or else he will be loyal to the one and despise the other. You cannot serve God and mammon." — *Luke 16:1–3, 10–13 (NKJV)*

What is an ERA? Well, it's like an IRA but only it's your Eternal Retirement Account. From this passage we learn some important truths about money. Jesus uses the story of a steward to show us that what we do with money matters far beyond the dollars and cents, it reflects our faithfulness and our loyalty.

Five Things We Learn About Money

1. **God Has More Than Enough** — "A certain rich man." God is the source, and His supply is never lacking.

2. **We Are Managers, Not Owners** — We are stewards of what belongs to God.

3. **We Shouldn't Waste It** — The steward was accused of wasting, and that was a serious charge.

4. **We Need a Plan** — The steward asked himself, *"What shall I do?"* A plan matters, especially when it comes to things like getting out of debt.

5. **Money Is a Test** — Jesus said that faithfulness with money reveals whether we can be trusted with true riches.

   > He who *is* faithful in *what is* least is faithful also in much; and he who is unjust in *what is* least is unjust also in much. Therefore if you have not been faithful in the unrighteous mammon, who will commit to your trust the true *riches?* — Luke 16:10–11 (NKJV)

There is a number in Scripture that often represents testing, and that is the number **10**.

- The 10 Commandments test our love for God and for others.

- In the parable of the 10 virgins, five were ready and five were not. That was a test of preparation.

- And in the same way, God uses the tithe—the first 10%, as a test of our trust.

> "Bring all the tithes into the storehouse, That there may be food in My house, And try Me now in this," says the Lord of hosts, "If I will not open for you the windows of heaven And pour out for you *such* blessing That *there will* not *be room* enough to *receive it*. And I will rebuke the devourer for your sakes, So that he will not destroy the fruit of your ground, Nor shall the vine fail to bear fruit for you in the field," Says the Lord of hosts. — *Malachi 3:10–11 (NKJV)*

Notice that God says, *"Try Me now in this."* Tithing is the one area where God invites us to put Him to the test.

1. What Is the Tithe?

The word *tithe* literally means "tenth." The tithe is the first tenth of our income.

An offering is anything above our tithe. For example: if I owed you $10 and gave you $5, then said, "Here's $10," you would have a problem with that. The tithe is not whatever we decide, it is specifically the tenth part.

> And all the tithe of the land, *whether* of the seed of the land or of the fruit of the tree, *is* the Lord's. It *is* holy to the Lord. — *Leviticus 27:30 (NKJV)*

Tithing Is Not Giving, But Returning

The tithe already belongs to the Lord. When we tithe, we are not giving God something new—we are returning what is His.

Think of it this way: if I borrowed your coat and then wrapped it up and gave it back to you at Christmas, you would not think much of that "gift." You would say, "That was mine already." That is what it is like when we bring the tithe—it was never ours to begin with.

Where Do We Bring the Tithe?

We are instructed to bring the tithe into the storehouse, which is God's house. In practical terms, this is the local church—the place where you are fed spiritually. We don't get to choose where we bring the tithe. God established that it was the temple (today local church) where He feeds and leads His people. After we tithe, we can decide where and how much we give.

Your tithe makes it possible for the gospel to be preached and for lives to be changed. It provides spiritual food for people who are hungry for the Word of God.

The First Portion Belongs to God

The tithe is given on the gross, not the net. It comes first, not after taxes or leftovers. God deserves the first portion. When we bring Him the first and best, we are declaring that everything we have comes from Him, and that we trust Him to provide for the rest.

2. Three Returns on The Tithe

We should always give with a higher motive than simply to get. Giving is first and foremost an act of worship, an acknowledgment that everything we have comes from God. Yet, God Himself doesn't hesitate to tell us about the benefits of our giving.

He actually delights in showing us the blessings tied to obedience.

#1 Guaranteed Gains

God promises that He will *"open for you the windows of heaven and pour out for you such blessing that there will not be room enough to receive it."* If Bill Gates were to open the windows of his checkbook to you, would you get excited? Then how much more should we rejoice when the Almighty God, the Creator of heaven and earth, says that He will open His windows of blessing over us?

This guarantee is so sure that God even says we can *test Him* in this matter. It is the only place in all of Scripture where the Lord invites us to test Him, and He even challenges us with it. It's almost as if He says, *"I dare you. Just try to prove Me wrong. Bring it on."*

History and testimony agree with this truth. John Templeton, chairman of Templeton Funds, once said:

"I have observed over 100,000 families over my years of investment counseling. I always saw greater prosperity and happiness among those families who tithed than among those who didn't."

Similarly, Mr. Kraft, founder of the Kraft Cheese Corporation, who gave nearly 25% of his income to Christian causes, declared:

"The only investment I ever made which has paid consistently increasing dividends is the money I have given to the Lord."

The world calls it generosity. God calls it obedience. And He guarantees that obedience unlocks blessing.

#2 Anti-Theft Protection

The Lord also promises that when we tithe, He will *rebuke the devourer* for our sake. In other words, He fights our money battles. He places His blessing on what we already have so that it lasts longer and accomplishes more. Think of it this way: God Himself becomes your personal Brinks security system, protecting your resources.

But if God rebukes the enemy when we give, doesn't it make sense that the devil will try to talk us out of giving? Every time we tithe, it's like God gives the enemy a black eye in the area of our finances.

We see an example of this in the story of Joshua and the battle at Ai.

Chapter 9: Stewardship — Faithfully Managing Time, Talent, and Treasure

> So the Lord said to Joshua... "Israel has sinned, and they have also transgressed My covenant which I commanded them. For they have even taken some of the accursed things, and have both stolen and deceived... Therefore the children of Israel could not stand before their enemies...'" — *Joshua 7:10–12 (NKJV)*

What were these "accursed things"? Before Israel conquered Jericho, God gave clear instructions:

> And you, by all means abstain from the accursed things, lest you become accursed when you take of the accursed things, and make the camp of Israel a curse, and trouble it. But all the silver and gold, and vessels of bronze and iron, *are* consecrated to the Lord; they shall come into the treasury of the Lord. — *Joshua 6:18–19 (NKJV)*

Jericho's wealth was not Israel's to take—it was set apart for God as first fruits. By bringing it into His house, He would remove the curse from what came out of pagan culture. But one man, Achan, disobeyed:

> Achan replied, "It is true! I have sinned against the LORD... Among the plunder I saw a beautiful robe from Babylon, 200 silver

coins, and a bar of gold... I wanted them so much that I took them." ... And all the Israelites stoned Achan ... Then piled a great heap of stones over Achan, which remains to this day..." — *Joshua 7:20-21, 25-26 (NLT)*

Doesn't this sound familiar? *"I saw it. I wanted it. So, I charged it."* Many today are living under a similar burden of debt. Achan ended up literally "aching" under a heap of stones.

Why did Jericho belong to God? Because Jericho was the *first fruits*—the tithe of the land—and the first always belongs to the Lord. By claiming it, God was not only honoring His rightful place as first but also removing the curse from what was tainted by paganism.

Tithing, then, isn't just about money—it's about alignment. It places our finances under God's blessing and protection instead of under the enemy's curse.

#3 Retirement Benefits

When you give, you are not just meeting a need in the present, you are making an investment in

Chapter 9: Stewardship — Faithfully Managing Time, Talent, and Treasure

eternity. You can't take your money with you when you leave this earth, but you can send it on ahead.

Jesus Himself taught us this principle:

> "Do not lay up for yourselves treasures on earth, where moth and rust destroy and where thieves break in and steal; but lay up for yourselves treasures in heaven, where neither moth nor rust destroys and where thieves do not break in and steal. For where your treasure is, there your heart will be also." — *Matthew 6:19–21 (NKJV)*

This is about perspective. Earthly wealth is fragile—it fades, it can be stolen, and it never truly satisfies. But when we give to God, we convert temporary resources into eternal treasure.

Famous new paper columnist Ann Landers once told the story of a girl who wrote about her aunt and uncle. She said her uncle was the stingiest person she had ever met. All his life, every time he got paid, he would slip $20 under his mattress. Then, when he became gravely ill and was about to die, he made his wife promise: *"When I die, take all the money under the mattress and bury it with me."*

After he died, his wife faithfully kept her word. On the day of the funeral, she emptied the mattress, took the money to the bank, deposited it, and wrote out a check. She placed the check in his casket. Promise kept.

When you stand in eternity, which do you think is more likely for you to say? *"I gave too much"* or *"I wish I had given more"*?

If you knew that tomorrow the American dollar would collapse and the only currency that would hold value was the Euro, what would you do? You'd exchange everything you had into the currency that lasts. That's exactly what giving does—it converts earthly currency, which will one day be worthless, into eternal currency that never loses value.

We see a living picture of this in the story of Elijah and the widow of Zarephath. Elijah, in the middle of a drought, was sent by God to a widow who had almost nothing left:

> So she said, "...I do not have bread, only a handful of flour in a bin, and a little oil in a jar; and see, I *am* gathering a couple of sticks that I may go in and prepare it for myself and my son, that we may eat it, and die." — *1 Kings 17:12 (NKJV)*

Elijah gave her a faith test:

> And Elijah said to her, "Do not fear; go *and* do as you have said, but make me a small cake from it first, and bring *it* to me; and afterward make *some* for yourself and your son. For thus says the Lord God of Israel: 'The bin of flour shall not be used up, nor shall the jar of oil run dry, until the day the Lord sends rain on the earth.'" — *1 Kings 17:13-14 (NKJV)*

She chose to give first. She trusted God with the little she had. And God made sure that her jar never ran dry.

That's what tithing is, it's trusting God first, and in return, experiencing His provision not only for today but also for tomorrow. It's retirement benefits in the truest sense—not just for this life, but for eternity.

3. Why Tithing Is Still New Testament

Many people ask, *"Isn't tithing just an Old Testament practice?"* But Scripture gives us clear reasons why tithing is still for today. In fact, the principle of putting God first with our finances is both eternal and essential. Let's look at seven reasons why tithing is still for the New Testament believer.

#1 Our Heart Follows Our Money

Jesus said it plainly:

> For where your treasure is, there your heart will be also. — *Matthew 6:21 (NKJV)*

If you want to know where your heart really is, look at your checkbook or your online bank statement. You can quickly tell if your treasure is at the mall or in God's house.

If I told my wife I loved her but insisted, *"Everything I have is mine,"* what would she think about my love? Love that doesn't share isn't love at all.

God made the same case to His people through Malachi:

> "Return to Me, and I will return to you," says the Lord of hosts. "But you said, 'In what way shall we return?' Will a man rob God? Yet you have robbed Me! But you say, 'In what way have we robbed You?' In tithes and offerings. You are cursed with a curse, for you have robbed Me, *Even* this whole nation." — *Malachi 3:7b–9 (NKJV)*

God was saying: *"Your heart has wandered. How do I know? You've stolen from Me in tithes and offerings."*

The tithe is always a test of the heart. As we mentioned earlier numbers in the Bible carry significance—3 is perfection, 7 is completion, 12 is divine government, and 10 is testing. Think about it:

- How many plagues tested Pharaoh's heart? **Ten.**

- How many commandments test our obedience to God? **Ten.**

- How many virgins were tested in Matthew 25? **Ten.**

Every time we get paid, God is testing our hearts with the number 10. *Will we put Him first?*

Sadly, statistics show that the average Christian gives only 2% of their income, and less than 3% of believers actually tithe. That means most are failing the test.

#2 God Is Always First

The first commandment makes this clear:

> You shall have no other gods before Me. — *Exodus 20:3 (NKJV)*

Jesus expanded this truth in Luke 16 when He said, *"You cannot serve God and mammon."* If God is not first in our money, then He is not first in our lives.

Why? Because nothing represents your life more than money. Life is measured in time, and when you run out of time, your life is over. You spend part of your life to earn money. That money then represents your life printed on paper or stored digitally. What you do with it reflects who and what you worship.

When we tithe, we are declaring: *"God, you are Lord over my life, because You are Lord over my money."*

The principle of God's first extends all through Scripture:

> Then the Lord spoke to Moses, saying, "Consecrate to Me all the firstborn, whatever opens the womb among the children of

> Israel, *both* of man and beast; it is Mine." — *Exodus 13:1 (NKJV)*

In the Old Testament, God asked Abraham to offer his firstborn son, Isaac. In the New Testament, God gave His own firstborn, Jesus. In a sense, Jesus was God's tithe—the first and best, given in faith before the harvest of souls was gathered.

The early church understood this as well. That's why believers met on Sunday—the first day of the week—to honor God first. God has always been first, and He will not come second to anyone or anything.

Have you ever wondered why God accepted Abel's offering but not Cain's?

> And in the process of time it came to pass that Cain brought an offering of the fruit of the ground to the Lord. Abel also brought of the firstborn of his flock and of their fat. And the Lord respected Abel and his offering, but He did not respect Cain and his offering. — *Genesis 4:3–5 (NKJV)*

Abel brought the firstborn—the first and best. Cain brought *"in the process of time"*—leftovers. God doesn't bless leftovers. He is worthy of our best.

That's what the tithe is: *putting God first, not last.* When we write the tithe check or set aside that first 10%, we are saying, *"God, I honor You before my mortgage company, before the electric bill, before the mall, and before my wants. You are first."*

#3 God Doesn't Change

When a new mother holds her child and whispers, *"Lord, will You help me?"* she is appealing to the unchanging character of God. He has always been faithful and always will be.

> "For I *am* the Lord, I do not change; Therefore you are not consumed, O sons of Jacob. Yet from the days of your fathers, You have gone away from My ordinances and have not kept *them*." — *Malachi 3:6 (NKJV)*

Notice that right before God speaks about the tithe, He reminds us: *"I do not change."* This is no coincidence. God places the eternal truth of His unchanging nature directly in the context of giving and putting Him first.

If God required it then, He requires it now. His character does not shift with culture, trends, or times.

Chapter 9: Stewardship — Faithfully Managing Time, Talent, and Treasure

#4 Tithing Predates the Law

Some say tithing was only part of the Old Testament law. But the reality is, tithing existed **long before the Law was ever given.**

More than 500 years before Moses, Abraham tithed to Melchizedek:

> Then Melchizedek king of Salem brought out bread and wine; he *was* the priest of God Most High. And he blessed him and said: "Blessed be Abram of God Most High, Possessor of heaven and earth; And blessed be God Most High, Who has delivered your enemies into your hand." And he gave him a tithe of all. — *Genesis 14:18–20 (NKJV)*

And 400 years before the Law, Jacob promised to give God a tenth of all his increase (Genesis 28:22). Clearly, tithing was never just about the Mosaic Law—it is a principle that transcends it.

In fact, in Abraham's story, notice the sequence: before Melchizedek (a clear picture of Christ) appears, the king of Sodom (a type of Satan) shows up.

> Now the king of Sodom said to Abram, "Give me the persons, and take the goods for yourself." — *Genesis 14:21 (NKJV)*

Do you see it? Satan's priority has always been the same: *"Give me the people. You can keep the stuff."* He doesn't care about possessions—they are temporary. What he wants are souls.

That's why tithing matters so much. When we withhold the tithe, we are buying into the lie of Sodom: *keep the stuff, forget the souls.* But when we tithe, we fund the mission of the church, which is the hope of the world.

Abraham's response is powerful:

> But Abram said to the king of Sodom, "I have raised my hand to the Lord, God Most High, the Possessor of heaven and earth, that I *will take* nothing, from a thread to a sandal strap, and that I will not take anything that *is* yours, lest you should say, 'I have made Abram rich.'" — *Genesis 14:22–23 (NKJV)*

Abraham refused to enrich himself from Sodom's hand. His source was the Lord alone.

Chapter 9: Stewardship — Faithfully Managing Time, Talent, and Treasure

The writer of Hebrews confirms that this moment wasn't about mere tradition—it pointed directly to Jesus:

> For this Melchizedek, king of Salem, priest of the Most High God, who met Abraham returning from the slaughter of the kings and blessed him, to whom also Abraham gave a tenth part of all, first being translated "king of righteousness," and then also king of Salem, meaning "king of peace," without father, without mother, without genealogy, having neither beginning of days nor end of life, but made like the Son of God, remains a priest continually. — *Hebrews 7:1–3 (NKJV)*

And then he makes the connection clear:

> Here mortal men receive tithes, but there he *receives them*, of whom it is witnessed that he lives. Even Levi, who receives tithes, paid tithes through Abraham, so to speak, for he was still in the loins of his father when Melchizedek met him. — *Hebrews 7:8–10 (NKJV)*

In other words, when we tithe, we are not simply giving to men or churches—we are giving to the eternal, living Christ, our High Priest who still receives tithes today.

#5 Jesus Endorsed Tithing

Jesus did not dismiss the tithe; rather, He affirmed it while calling His followers to an even higher standard of righteousness.

> "Woe to you, scribes and Pharisees, hypocrites! For you pay tithe of mint and anise and cummin, and have neglected the weightier *matters* of the law: justice and mercy and faith. These you ought to have done, without leaving the others undone." — *Matthew 23:23 (NKJV)*

Notice, Jesus didn't say, *"Stop tithing, that's Old Testament law."* Instead, He said they should have done the weightier matters without leaving the others undone. In other words, tithing was still right, but their hearts also needed to be aligned with justice, mercy, and faith.

In fact, Jesus consistently elevated the standard of righteousness. The law said, *"Do not murder,"* but Jesus said, *"Whoever hates in his heart commits murder."* The law said, *"Do not commit adultery,"* but Jesus said, *"Whoever lusts in his heart has already committed adultery."* Far from lowering the bar, Jesus raised it.

Chapter 9: Stewardship — Faithfully Managing Time, Talent, and Treasure

Consider also the parable of the Pharisee and the tax collector:

> "Two men went up to the temple to pray, one a Pharisee and the other a tax collector. The Pharisee stood by himself and prayed: 'God, I thank you that I am not like other people—robbers, evildoers, adulterers—or even like this tax collector. I fast twice a week and give a tenth of all I get.'" — *Luke 18:10–12 (NIV)*

Here, Jesus acknowledged that the Pharisee's tithing was a righteous act. The problem was not the tithe—it was his pride.

In contrast, the tax collector humbled himself before God:

> "But the tax collector stood at a distance. He would not even look up to heaven, but beat his breast and said, 'God, have mercy on me, a sinner.' I tell you that this man, rather than the other, went home justified before God. For all those who exalt themselves will be humbled, and those who humble themselves will be exalted." — *Luke 18:13–14 (NIV)*

Jesus showed us that tithing without humility misses the heart of worship but tithing with humility honors God and advances His kingdom.

#6 The Tithe Was Used for Ministry

What was the tithe used for in the Old Testament? It provided for the temple, sustained the priests, and ensured the Word of God was taught to the people.

Does God still have a house that carries out this mission? Absolutely—today it is called the church. And our mission is even greater: not just serving one nation but carrying the gospel to the ends of the earth.

Would God give the church a greater vision and then remove the provision for it? Certainly not. The principle of the tithe remains the means by which God funds His work through His people.

7# Why the Tithe Is Not Directly Commanded in the New Testament

Some ask why the New Testament doesn't contain a direct command to tithe. The answer lies in how Jesus taught.

> "Therefore I speak to them in parables, because seeing they do not see, and hearing they do not hear, nor do they understand. And in them the prophecy of Isaiah is fulfilled, which says: 'Hearing you will hear and shall not understand, And seeing you will see and not perceive; For the hearts of this people have grown dull. *Their* ears are hard of hearing, And their eyes they have closed, Lest they should see with *their* eyes and hear with *their* ears, lest they should understand with *their* hearts and turn, so that I should heal them.'" — *Matthew 13:13–15 (NKJV)*

Jesus often concealed truth in parables, revealing it only to those whose hearts were truly seeking Him. The principle of tithing is not abolished—it is woven into the fabric of Scripture, from Abraham to Jesus Himself.

The New Testament does not emphasize tithing as a legalistic duty but assumes it as a spiritual practice, while calling us into an even deeper generosity motivated by love, faith, and obedience.

About the Author

Erik Lawson is the founding pastor of Element Church, a congregation of more than 5,000 with its main campus located in Wentzville, Missouri. He is known for his dynamic communication style and in-depth Bible teaching communicated with practical life application. In addition to his role as the senior pastor of a multi-site local church, and a world-wide online presence with Element Everywhere, he has an insightful leadership podcast called *All Out Leadership* and is a one-on-one leadership coach to pastors.

Prior to founding Element Church he led what was at the time, the largest youth group in America, Church on The Move's nationally acclaimed, Oneighty©, with as many as 3,000 young people attending each week.

Erik lives in Wentzville, Missouri with his wife Sunny. He is the father of three wonderful adult children and has three beautiful granddaughters. In his free time, Erik enjoys spending time reading, hunting and fishing, playing Fortnite with friends, going for walks in the park with Sunny, and eating ice cream.

www.ingramcontent.com/pod-product-compliance
Lightning Source LLC
LaVergne TN
LVHW020927090426
835512LV00020B/3237